Reading and Interpreting the Works of

JACK LONDON

Enslow Publishing
101 W. 23rd Street
Suite 240
New York, NY 10011
USA

enslow.com

Lit Crit Guides

Reading and Interpreting the Works of

JACK
LONDON

Stephanie
Buckwalter

Published in 2018 by Enslow Publishing, LLC
101 W. 23rd Street, Suite 240, New York, NY 10011

Cataloging-in-Publication Data
Title: Reading and interpreting the works of Jack London / Stephanie Buckwalter.
Description: New York : Enslow Publishing, 2018 | Series: Lit crit guides | Includes bibliographical references and index. | Audience: Grades 7-12.
Identifiers: ISBN 9780766084919 (library bound)
Subjects: LCSH: London, Jack, 1876-1916--Criticism and interpretation--Juvenile literature. | London, Jack, 1876-1916--Juvenile literature.
Classification: LCC PS3523.O46 Z614 2018 | DDC 813/.52--dc23

Printed in China

10 9 8 7 6 5 4 3 2 1

To Our Readers: We have done our best to make sure all website addresses in this book were active and appropriate when we went to press. However, the author and the publisher have no control over and assume no liability for the material available on those websites or on any websites they may link to. Any comments or suggestions can be sent by email to customerservice@enslow.com.

Portions of this book originally appeared in *A Student's Guide to Jack London.*

CONTENTS

Jack London

LOOKING THROUGH A KALEIDOSCOPE

Jack London's life story reads like that of the mythical American hero. He lived out the rags-to-riches stories he read as a child and pursued adventure wherever it could be found. As a writer, he possessed the uncanny ability to capture the essence of an experience and, with a little imagination, turn it into interesting reading. Because of his tendency to romanticize his real-life experiences, reading London is like looking through a kaleidoscope, seeing bits and pieces of his life reflected in his fiction. One scholar, Alfred Kazin, even wrote, "The greatest story Jack London ever wrote was the story he lived."[1]

Biographers often struggle with categorizing London's body of work. As one biographer puts it, "Trying to pinpoint a consistent philosophy in London's work fails."[2] One reason is because London used his writing for many things: to make money, to relive/rewrite his experiences and life story, to promote the socialist cause, and to promote his own philosophies. Another reason is that London was a voracious reader. He sought after the writings of the great thinkers of his day. As he read, he incorporated new ideas into his work. Both his purpose for writing and his philosophy of life were moving targets.

London went through three major life changes. Each time, he added a new dimension to his life's philosophy—or changed it completely. First, his childhood work in the factories and his experience as a hobo gave birth to his identity as a socialist. Second, his trip to the Klondike convinced him that he should be a writer rather than work at manual labor or pursue a trade. Third, his disenchantment with the capitalist system represented by factories and the working poor created a desire to return to the land as a farmer. It is not surprising, then, that his contributions to his era fall into three areas: political, literary, and agricultural.

Age of Transition

Jack London lived in a time of rapid social change. The Industrial Age in America was in full swing during his adult years. Immigrants were flooding into America, creating a cheap labor pool to populate the factories. Many Americans were moving from rural areas to cities to work in factories. This mass movement created a political shift as well. The farmer was no longer the driver of the American economy. Big business, in the form of corporations and trusts, was influencing politicians and economic policy.

WHAT IS A KALEIDOSCOPE?

A kaleidoscope is a cylinder with bits and pieces of glass or beads that are reflected in mirrors. The arrangement of the bits and pieces are random, but the reflection, repeated by the mirrors, makes them appear symmetrical. The end piece of the kaleidoscope can be twisted slightly to form an always-changing view of the pieces. In similar fashion, reading Jack London is like looking through a kaleidoscope. The bits and pieces are his adventures, philosophies, relationships, writing skills, and imagination. As time goes on, with each new adventure or philosophy encountered, his shifting views can be seen in his writing.

These societal changes had a great influence on London, who spent his earliest years living on farms and then in the city. In his youth, he labored in the factories for ten cents an hour. He shoveled coal for an unscrupulous boss who paid him the salary of one man while he did the work of two. These experiences profoundly shaped his attitudes about society and created a strong desire to rise above his working-class status.

At one point, London became a hobo. During this time he was introduced to the ideas of Karl Marx and socialism. Marx proposed "the abolition of private property in land; abolition of all rights of inheritance; factories, means of production, communication, and transportation to be owned by the state; and all wealth, except consumption goods, to be owned collectively."[3] When London combined his personal experience in the factories with the philosophies of Karl Marx, he grasped the essence of the socialist movement: the belief that big business taking advantage of the common worker was a hopeless system. He firmly believed that socialism was the answer to the gross abuses he saw in the factories.

London wrote frequently for the socialist cause in newsletters and magazines and gave speeches and lectures across the country. *The Iron Heel*, a novel about a socialist revolt in a futuristic society, was one of London's literary attempts to promote the cause of socialism. Unfortunately, London's tendency toward violence and gore did not match up well with the socialist's agenda of a bloodless revolution through propaganda. The socialists did not really like it.

A Convergence of Writing, Printing, and Marketing

London had an immense talent for writing short stories, and he had incredible luck in getting his stories into the marketplace. He was the right person with the right skills at just the right time in history. The publishing industry was exploding and London got in on the ground floor.

The rise of industrialization gave rise to the age of magazines. The magazine industry in America reached its height at the end of the nineteenth century. From 1890 to 1915, the golden age of magazines, magazine production flourished. Mass circulation, facilitated by the expanding rail system, allowed people to get news and new ideas from all over the United States. Initially, magazine content was geared toward the cultured upper classes, but newer magazines catered

London at his desk at Beauty Ranch

to the unrefined masses. Those masses now had access to book serializations and reviews, political commentary, celebrity gossip (including London's latest exploits), and stories of national importance.

> **short story**
>
> A fictional narrative that focuses on a single incident or a very short period of time.

The golden age of magazines gave rise to the age of advertising. Magazines were primarily financed by paid subscriptions, usually purchased by middle-class Americans. But the majority of the funding to pay writers came from advertising. With industrialization and mass production, companies needed to find markets for all the goods coming off the production lines. Magazines were the perfect vehicle for advertising. Companies were willing to pay large sums of money to place ads in popular magazines.

Although marketing data as we know it today was not available, magazine owners had a good idea of their market and catered to them. The Victorian Age was coming to an end. There was a high demand for writers who could produce adventure stories to catch the public's interest. Part of this taste for adventure can be attributed to President Theodore Roosevelt (president from 1901–1909). An avid outdoorsman and member of the Rough Riders during the Spanish-American War, he exuded vitality and energy—the embodiment of rugged individualism.

Short stories in particular were in demand. They fit the magazine spacing format and could be read in one sitting.[4] Short stories tend to isolate a single person or moment and examine it, focusing on inward personal qualities. London studied the market and gave the publishers and the public what they wanted. He mastered the short story and wrote about his own adventures, giving them a realism that attracted a wide audience.

In addition to publishing short stories, magazines serialized novels, publishing one book chapter in each issue. Once the last chapter was published, a traditional publisher would release the novel in book form. Serialization gave the author the opportunity to attract a wider audience and to make more money— first with the magazine, then with a publisher. Using this model, London's full-length novels were serialized and his short stories were collected into books after they appeared

serialization

Publishing a story in parts at regular intervals. Magazines often serialized novels by printing a new chapter in each issue.

Teddy Roosevelt and the Rough Riders stand on the hill that they captured at the Battle of San Juan in 1898.

in magazines. He worked the system well, becoming the first American author to make a million dollars from writing.

Literary Friends

London claimed that he learned his craft without the help and support of like-minded individuals, but he moved in literary circles that included many of the artists and writers popular in his day. His home, Beauty Ranch, became a hotspot for creative types in and around San Francisco. People could drop in and stay, with complete access to his ranch. His only request was that his guests respect his work time every morning; play came in the afternoon. His hospitality was well known and appreciated by his friends and visitors.

London's local friends included George Sterling, a poet who became a close friend and confidant. He critiqued London's manuscripts and even worked on *Martin Eden*. Sterling was a good friend of Ambrose Bierce, best known for his short story "An Occurrence at Owl Creek Bridge." Although Sterling and Bierce were close, London could not tolerate Bierce, so the three were seldom together except on rare social occasions.

Victorian Age

The time of Queen Victoria's reign over the United Kingdom (1837–1901).

London had correspondence and personal meetings with several literary figures of the time. In 1910 and 1911, when Sinclair Lewis was just starting out, London purchased plot outlines from him. Lewis later went on to become the first American to win the Nobel Prize in Literature.

London also corresponded with Upton Sinclair. He wrote a review of *The Jungle* as a personal favor for Sinclair. Several

London (*second from right*) sits with his friend George Sterling (*far left*) and writers Mary Austin and James Hopper.

of London's letters to Sinclair from 1910 to 1916 can be read online at the Huntington Library website.[5]

London once wrote to Joseph Conrad after reading Conrad's *Victory*, commenting on how much he admired it. In countries like Norway and Sweden, Conrad was considered a literary type of Jack London. Conrad's novel, *The Heart of Darkness*, was set in the jungle with cannibals, akin to London's South Seas stories. Conrad did not agree with this comparison. He thought London's writing was more sensationalist than his own.[6]

Facets of London's Kaleidoscope

Any discussion of London's work will include controversy and contradictions. London was a man of his times. The times were changing and so was he. In his early years he supported socialism. Later in life he became a practicing capitalist. He held to the idea of white racial superiority yet often elevated the underdog in his stories. His early naturalistic plots eventually gave way to more spiritually centered stories. In many ways, London was ahead of his time. He supported the era's New Woman: a woman who was empowered, independent, and free of society's traditional expectations for women. London supported women's suffrage and prohibition. He promoted American imperialism. And like President Roosevelt, he advocated land reuse and soil conservation.

Writing His Current Philosophy

Critics and scholars agree that London's Klondike writings, including the short story "To Build a Fire" and novel *The Call of the Wild*, are among his best works. (The Klondike is a region of Canada along the Klondike River, just east of Alaska.) His experiences there gave focus to his writing. His vivid depictions of life in the Northland draw readers into the story. These are the stories that brought him worldwide fame.

London eventually grew tired of writing about the Klondike, but his readers clamored for more. He obliged at first, but quickly expanded into other areas such as reporting and nonfiction books. London's Hawaiian stories were received well enough, as were his short stories from the South Seas. But London ran into trouble when he wrote novels, partly because his work was rarely simple entertainment.

London often wrote to espouse an ideology or his current philosophy, or to carry out a personal agenda. He admitted, "I will sacrifice form every time, when it boils down to a final question of choice between form and matter. The thought is the thing."[7] He willingly sacrificed the form of novel writing to get his philosophical points across.

Because of London's tendency to preach his life's philosophy through his stories, many of his later books received only lukewarm receptions from contemporary critics. However, modern scholarship looks at the late stories differently, taking into account the philosophical and cultural content only evident from the perspective of history. Modern scholars also have access to a huge store of London's personal papers, correspondence, and annotated books from his personal library. Comparing his writing to his personal notes reveals a lot of what drove London in his writing at any given time. These more intimate looks into the man were not available to his contemporary critics.

Themes of Intellect and Instinct

Much of London's early work falls into the category of naturalism. Naturalism as a literary genre was shaped by the emerging discoveries and theories of science. Naturalism assumes a person's life is determined strictly by his surroundings and genetics. The individual does not have a spirit but lives completely within the physical realm of nature. This style is particularly evident in London's Klondike stories, where nature is depicted as an antagonist and much of the action includes the interaction between man and nature.

As an extension of naturalism, London liked to intertwine intellect and instinct. He masters this interplay in *The Call of the Wild*, where the dog Buck comes into the wilderness with intellect but has to develop his instincts. London identifies the intellect with civilization and instinct with the wilderness. This interplay is also evident in *White Fang*. The dog White Fang functions mainly on instinct in the wilderness but develops intellectually as he is drawn farther and farther into the civilized world.

London also promoted his views on social Darwinism, the idea that Darwin's theory of evolution can be applied to whole societies.[8] London believed that just as animals evolve, societies evolve. He plays out this theme in many of his Klondike stories. For example, to survive in the Northland, one "must be prepared to forget many of the things he has learned, and to acquire such customs as are inherent with existence in the new land; . . . and oftentimes he must reverse the very codes by which his conduct has hitherto been shaped."[9] In London's Northland, if a person does not adapt to his new society, he fails. This failure inevitably leads to death, leaving only those best able to adapt to carry on in society.

> **naturalism**
>
> A style of fiction in which a character's life is determined strictly by his surroundings and genetics. The individual does not have a spirit but lives completely within the physical realm of nature.

Charles Darwin

Social Darwinism, taken to its logical conclusion, leads to the idea that through natural selection there is a hierarchy of societies. Social Darwinists usually identified societies by race. London promoted the idea of Anglo-Saxon superiority to justify American imperialism.[10] Even though he held to these beliefs, he often found that which was admirable in these so-called inferior races. His portrayal of Indians in the Klondike shows his sensitivity to their plight of losing their homeland to the settlers. Still later, in his Hawaiian fiction, London demonstrates empathy for the islanders who lost their lands to the invading British.

Although death is not a theme in London's works, he never shied away from depicting it in his writings, often making a character's death central to the progression of the story. Because of the vivid depictions of violence and gore, he earned the title "Father of Red-Blooded American Literature."[11] *The Call of the Wild* is filled with red imagery, from the red sweater of Buck's first tamer to the red blood in Buck's mouth as he kills his prey in the final chapter. White Fang, too, becomes a master at drawing blood from his enemies.

A typical example of London's prose is the description of the seal slaughter in *The Sea-Wolf*: "After a good day's killing I have seen our decks covered with hides and bodies, slippery with fat and blood, the scuppers running red; masts, ropes, and rails spattered with the sanguinary color; and the men, like butchers plying their trade, naked and red of arm and hand, hard at work with ripping and flensing knives, removing the skins from the pretty sea creatures they had killed."[12] Although the char-

Darwinism

The theory of evolution through natural selection popularized by Charles Darwin in his book *Origin of the Species*.

acter in the book is appalled by the gore, it is the writer who seems to like it.

Brawn, Brains, and Nature as Character Types

The significant themes in London's writing can be analyzed by tracing the social, physical, and psychological changes in his main characters. An overall analysis of his work shows that his main concerns tended to be class issues, reflecting his own rise from the working class to the middle class; physical beauty, strength, and intellect as signs of superiority; and nature as antagonist or healing retreat.

London's heroes are often supermen, using brawn or intellect to accomplish their purpose. The main character either possesses these traits when introduced, or the plot is about how the main character acquires them. For example, Humphrey Van Weyden in *The Sea-Wolf* acquires brawn and Martin Eden, in the novel of the same name, refines his intellect. This interplay between brawn and intellect probably comes from London's own experiences as he moved from working in the factories to becoming more of an intellectual.

Another element in London's writing is the feminist heroine, embodied in the era's New Woman. London's heroines, such as Frona Welse in *A Daughter of the Snows*, demonstrate great physical prowess.[13] This was shocking to the Victorian mind accustomed to the pure, protected, virginal heroines of the late-nineteenth-century novels.

London's second wife, Charmian Kitteredge, was the embodiment of the New Woman. She and London were equals in their relationship, an uncommon arrangement in that day and age. Each of London's Anglo-Saxon heroines created after he met her is a reflection of Charmian in some way.

London had the unique ability to write about nature in such a way as to give it a life and character of its own. He animates the dead of winter as the White Silence in his Klondike stories and makes nature the main character in his story "All Gold Canyon." This type of characterization fit in well with his penchant for naturalism.

Using Setting to Show Story Progression

London also used nature powerfully in setting. Through vivid description, he could intensify the

> **irony**
>
> The use of words to express an idea or ideas that are the opposite of the words' literal meaning.

narrative, provide a sensory experience, or foreshadow events in a story. A lot of his stories depend heavily upon a specific geographic location for effect, whether on the open sea, on a hot tropical island, in the frozen Northland, or in a peaceful California valley. And because most of his stories take place about the time he was alive, his settings provide breadth and depth to modern historical interpretations of his work.

Literary Devices as Intellectual Play

Irony and hyperbole both play roles in London's writing. He often uses irony to show the insensitivity of American imperialists as they took over land and people. Sometimes his irony hit a nerve and he suffered for revealing some of the activities taking place during

> **hyperbole**
>
> Bold overstatement for ironic or comic effect.

the process. However, he never apologized for his stories, claiming the right of an author to tell a good story.

London's most famous work, *The Call of the Wild*, uses anthropomorphism, giving human characteristics to animals. By using animals, he allows the reader to regress along with Buck from civilization to the wild. The reader can easily apply the process to humans, but the sheer brutality of the humans to the dogs and the dogs to each other is easier to accept when observed in the animal world.

Contrast was a favorite tool for London. He liked to show processes in reverse, or the flip side of character under pressure. Instead of using contrast within stories, he would conceive two entirely different stories. *The Call of the Wild*, in which a tame dog from California regresses to the wild, is in complete contrast to *White Fang*, the story of a wild dog from the Yukon being tamed. In his book of short stories, *The Son of the Wolf*, the half-breed Malemute Kid is contrasted with lesser men like Carter Weatherbee and Percy Cuthfert. The Kid lives by a code of ethics based on survival and camaraderie. Weatherbee and Cuthfert end up killing each other during the White Silence of a Yukon winter because of selfishness.

Real-Life Fiction

Jack London's personal experiences brought to his writing a realism that was lacking in the short stories typical of the late 1800s. He directed his stories to his audience: the working class. His plain talk and direct, sometimes violent, depictions of events contrasted sharply with the Victorian romance novel.

Several factors played into the making of Jack London both as a man and a writer: poverty, his many adventures, manual labor in various factories, time in jail, and a trip to the Yukon. He had the gift of turning the meat of his experiences into fiction, making them come alive for many who would never experience these things themselves. His audience loved it.

PIECES OF PERSONAL HISTORY

Pieces of London's early life found their way into the kaleidoscope of his writing. His late teens, especially, were full of activity and adventure. These pieces of his life would show up in his later works, after he established himself by writing about the Klondike.

Jack London was born in San Francisco, California, on January 12, 1876, as John Griffith Chaney. His mother, Flora Wellman, claimed that William H. Chaney was his father. Flora and Chaney had been living together at the time of conception, but Chaney deserted Flora soon after she announced she was pregnant, denying he was the father. After the birth, Flora was too weak to nurse Jack so she hired a wet nurse (a woman to breastfeed Jack in her place), Virginia "Jennie" Prentiss. Jennie became a surrogate mother for Jack, providing the love and comfort his mother would not. Jack visited Jennie often during his youth and they became lifelong friends.

On the Farm

Eight months after Jack was born, Flora married a Civil War veteran, John London. Until this time, Jack had been living with the Prentisses. When Flora remarried, Jack came to live with his mother, John, and John's two young daughters, Eliza and Ida. Eliza, only eight at the time, did most of the mothering for Jack during his childhood. Jack turned to her throughout his life for advice and other help.

Jack, age nine

Jack's stepfather, John, tried his hand at farming and was somewhat successful with a small plot of land in Oakland. At Flora's urging, they moved to a larger farm in the country. After several starts at various farms, each bigger than the last, they ran into hard times and lost everything. Like many others during the Industrial Age, they moved to the city to find work.

On the Bay

When Jack was about nine years old, the family returned to Oakland. They lived in poverty, frequently moving from house to house as necessity dictated. Jack's childhood days consisted of school, work, and fighting. While Jack attended school, he worked various jobs to supplement the family income. He worked as a newsboy, loaded ice wagons, swept saloons, and set up pins in a bowling alley. He also learned to fight. He was known as a solid fighter and needed only the slightest provocation to spark a brawl.

In Oakland, Jack discovered a treasure—the Oakland Free Library. The librarian, Ina Coolbrith, took a personal interest in Jack's intellectual development and helped guide him to suitable books to read. She describes Jack as "coming into the library with a bundle of newspapers under his arm, badly poised, looking poor, shabby, and uncared for, asking for something good to read, and wanting to consume every book that had an interesting title."[1] Some of his first books were Washington Irving's *Tales of the Alhambra* and Horatio Alger's stories. These adventure and rags-to-riches stories fanned the flames of Jack's desire to move up the social ladder and out of his narrow world.

Jack read voraciously while walking to and from school, while eating, and any time of day he could. Later in life, he observed that there were probably very few books in that library that were not, at one time or another, checked out under the name Jack London. He told his sister he wanted to one day have a house with one whole room devoted to books. He eventually ended up with several rooms of books.

Another of Jack's loves was the water. He began sailing with his stepfather around San Francisco Bay at a young age. By twelve years old, he could competently maneuver his skiff (a small rowboat with a sail) around the bay. He finished eighth grade at Cole Grammar School, but since the family needed money, he went to work in a cannery (a canning factory), putting an end to his formal schooling. The hours at the factory were long and grueling. Although only fourteen years old by this time, Jack developed a strong dislike for the mind-numbing life of a "work beast." To escape the drudgery, he turned to the taverns along the waterfront. Here he picked up the habit of drinking and heard fascinating stories from the men who worked the seas. He began to make a distinction in his mind between those he considered to be real men who really "lived" and those who stayed in the cities, bound to mindless work in the factories or growing soft in the genteel classes. These class distinctions would come to play an important part in many of his works.

Jack soon left the cannery to pursue adventure out on the bay. He borrowed three hundred dollars from Jenny Prentiss and bought a boat called the *Razzle Dazzle*. He became a juvenile delinquent, raiding private oyster beds. In those days, the railroad companies held monopolies on many businesses. They owned the rights to harvest oysters in San Francisco Bay. Deciding this was unfair, some men took to raiding the oyster beds and selling the oysters to the waterfront bars and markets for large profits. The railroad monopolies were not well liked, so public opinion favored the oyster pirates.

After about three months, the mainsail of his sloop burned in an accidental fire. Jack opted to join the California Fish Patrol, enforcing the law against the very people he used to work with. He found that his new associates drank even more than his pirating buddies, and he joined right in. In his sober moments, he began to see the need for a change of direction in his life.

Out to Sea

In 1893, Jack signed on to the *Sophia Sutherland* as an able-bodied seaman for an eight-month sealing voyage. The trip took him to Hawaii, the Bonin Islands, Japan, and the Bering Sea. Jack finally had his chance to see the world that

Inside Hickmott Canning Company, where Jack worked as a teenager

he had only read about. The ports, indeed, were exotic, but the up-close view of killing seals for profit balanced out Jack's romantic views of seafaring. His attitude toward sealing shows through the comments of Humphrey Van Weyden in *The Sea-Wolf*. "It was wanton slaughter, and all for woman's sake."[2] The seal fur was used to make women's clothing.

On the sea Jack learned the value of daily discipline and routine, which he incorporated into his professional life as a writer. When he finally began to write for a living, he committed to write one thousand words a day, regardless of his health or where he was at the time. By keeping this commitment he was able to produce fifty books and hundreds of short stories, essays, and articles in just sixteen years.

In the Labor Force

Upon return from the sea voyage, Jack came to realize that most of his former friends were either dead, in jail, or hiding from the law. And he wanted to live. Jack determined to change his life but faced the reality of a nationwide depression. Factories closed, banks folded, and thousands were without jobs. He returned to being a work beast, working in a jute mill making ropes for ten cents an hour.

During this time, his mother noticed a contest in the *San Francisco Morning Call* newspaper for youth writers. She encouraged Jack to enter. He did, writing a story titled "Story of a Typhoon Off the Coast of Japan," based on his experiences aboard the *Sophia Sutherland*. With only an eighth-grade education he won first prize: twenty-five dollars and publication in the newspaper. The second and third place winners were college students from the University of California and Stanford University. This was Jack's first experience with turning his life experiences into cash. Many of his youthful adventures would resurface in his writing, turning his life into stories.

During the Industrial Age, the general belief was that anyone could move up in a company through hard, honest work, rising through the ranks to one day become a partner in the firm. Believing this and having the good fortune to find a foreman with the same views, Jack took a job shoveling coal in a power plant. His boss indicated that within a couple of years Jack could achieve his dream. However, after a few weeks of intense manual labor, Jack found out his boss had deceived him. He was doing the work of two men and being paid the wages of one. He quit immediately, angry and disillusioned. He now became one of the tens of thousands of unemployed workers in the United States. At eighteen, he was lower on the socioeconomic scale than when he had started working.

With the Socialist Movement

London decided to join Jacob Coxey's Industrial Army, a nationwide rally of unemployed men who planned to march on the capital in Washington, DC. London caught up with the California contingent in the Sierra Nevada Mountains, traveling as a hobo on the rails as he had learned two years earlier from a group of homeless youth. While moving east with these men, London heard many discussions about socialism versus capitalism. He sided with the socialist point of view, agreeing with the idea that capitalism ignored the human needs of the masses in the interests of a greedy few at the top. He had already experienced the bottom of the Social Pit, as he called it, and could identify with those near the bottom of the social hierarchy.

Like many others facing this long march without much food or shelter, London deserted Coxey's Army. He went to

Chicago, visiting some of his mother's relatives before moving on to New York and Niagara Falls. After a single visit to the falls and one night in a field, he was arrested for vagrancy, or homelessness. The judge, accustomed to many of these types of arrests, showed no mercy and sentenced him to thirty days on a chain gang at the Erie County Penitentiary.

Here, London saw first-hand the awful conditions of US prisons of that time. There were no human rights considered. The castoffs of society ended up here, enduring brutality and degradation in a world governed by might. People got what they wanted through sheer physical force. It was here

Jacob Coxey (*center*) and his Industrial Army marched from Ohio to Washington, DC, to protest unemployment.

THE IMPACT OF LONDON'S SOCIALISM

Jack London's identity as a socialist provided some unique opportunities. In his early twenties, London began giving speeches on the subject and was known around Oakland as the Boy Socialist. He ran for mayor of Oakland, California, two times as the Socialist Party candidate but never won.

When fellow author and socialist Upton Sinclair was writing his novel *The Jungle*, London wrote a review for him.[3] Sinclair and London hoped to bring the plight of the worker into the spotlight. Instead, the novel brought about changes in the meat packing industry in particular through the Meat Inspection Act and the food industry in general through the Pure Food and Drug Act of 1906.

The Call of the Wild was one of a very few American books allowed to be read in the Soviet Union. Because of London's socialist writings and background, his work was not only allowed in Russia, it was required reading, as one visitor to Jack London State Park informed the docent.[4] London eventually resigned from the Socialist Party in 1916.

that London became convinced that salvation for the masses would come from socialism, and for the individual through intellectual power. He resolved "to sell no more muscle, and to become a vendor of brains."[5] He decided that education was the best way to achieve this goal.

At School

When London returned to Oakland in 1895, he enrolled in high school at the age of nineteen. He stayed for about a year before dropping out. During his time in high school he joined the Henry Clay Club (a debating club), befriended Herman

"Jim" Whitaker, who taught him boxing and fencing, and was frequently published in the school magazine, the *High School Aegis*. He also returned to the Oakland Free Library, where he came across a copy of Karl Marx's *Communist Manifesto*. He quickly identified with Marx's philosophy of rule by the working class rather than rule by the factory owners and big businessmen. His experiences at work and with poverty fostered a zeal for social reform, a theme that appears frequently in his writing. In 1896 he joined the Socialist Labor Party and became known for his fiery speeches in the public squares.

London's interest in politics and his foray into his own intellectual development opened a new world to him—middle-class society. He was invited into the homes of those who sympathized with the socialist cause. One family in particular took him in: the Applegarths, whose daughter, Mabel, became the model for the love interest in *Martin Eden*.

After his high school experience, London decided to attend college. Since he had not completed high school, he entered into an intense program of self-study. "I was working to get away from work," he reflected, "and I buckled down to it with the grim realization of the paradox."[6] He passed the entrance exams for the University of California, Berkeley. It was here that he read Herbert Spencer's books that tied Darwin's theory of evolution to social processes. Spencer's idea came to be known as social Darwinism, the idea that societies evolve, with the result that some are superior to others.

London soon realized that at twenty years old, he had more life experience than most of his professors and he was learning more on his own. He came to the conclusion that it was not worth trying to attend school and support his family members. After one semester, London dropped out of the university.

When he left Berkeley, London decided to try to make a living as a writer. He had had many discussions on becoming a writer with his friends in the debating club. He rented a type-writer and threw himself wholeheartedly into the endeavor. For months, the rejection slips piled up. No one was buying what he had to sell. Out of money, he went to work in the laundry of a military school, once again entering the ranks of the work beast. He was saved from this drudgery by a surprise twist of fate.

In the Klondike

Gold! The Klondike Gold Rush was on. During the summer of 1896, a group of miners discovered rich gold deposits in the rivers of Canada's Yukon Territory. Miners already in the area rushed to stake claims along the rivers. When some of these miners arrived in San Francisco on July 15 and in Seattle on July 17, 1897, it set off a stampede for America's last great gold rush. Jack London heard the call and turned to his sister for backing.

Eliza's husband, Captain James H. Shepard, agreed to go north with London to seek their fortunes. Eliza and Captain Shepard funded the venture by mortgaging their home and using their savings. London and Shepard started their journey in the summer of 1897.

Only two months into the deal, Shepard decided he was not up to this adventure physically and left London with supplies and money to finish the trip without him. London staked a claim near Dawson, where he stayed during the long Arctic winter. Biographer Stasz notes, "The Yukon would further test him and refine his materialistic bent…Ultimately,

Dawson, Alaska, during the Gold Rush in the late 1800s

Nature ruled, and she was no gentle goddess strewing flowers in the sunshine and sending rainbows after showers. Survival required cooperation, a theme that would resonate throughout most of his writings and reinforce his socialistic leanings."[7]

It was during this long winter that London came to grips with his life. He wrote, "It was in the Klondike that I found myself. There, nobody talks. Everybody thinks. You get your perspective. I got mine."[8] He made up his mind to pursue his dreams instead of returning to a life of manual labor. He left the Yukon Territory as soon as the spring thaw occurred, suffering from scurvy, a disease caused by a lack of vitamin C. He already had the early symptoms of swollen, bleeding gums and loose teeth. This would be the first of many instances where health problems cut his adventures short.

Most of London's stories have some elements of personal experience to them. London romanticized many of his physical hardships and challenges in his stories. For example, he described his actual experience going through the White Horse Rapids in his article "Through the Rapids on the Way to Klondike." The romanticized version appears in his book *Smoke Bellew*.[9]

This intense, one-year period accounts for London's second life change. London's transformation occurred during the long, sunless winter he describes in his stories as the White Silence. During this phase London did not find gold, but he acquired a gold mine of material for his future as a writer. He told stories and listened to the stories of others, both travelers and locals, stoking the fire of his imagination. The Klondike proved a rich source for the early success that would bring him worldwide fame.

Pieces of the Northland

L ondon's trip to the Klondike added the most important pieces to the kaleidoscope, the ones that provided for his early fame and fortune. Although the body of his work has many facets, the remainder of his career and his enduring legacy as an American author rests on the Klondike stories.

Upon returning home in June 1898, London found out his stepfather had died. He was now responsible for supporting his entire household. London took the civil service exam and applied for a job at the post office. While waiting to hear the results, he determined to pursue his dreams and resolved to try writing again.

Emerging from the White Silence

In 1898 London published more than twenty pieces of writing, mostly articles. He sent manuscripts to the magazines *Youth's Companion*, *Black Cat*, and the *Overland Monthly*. *Youth's Companion* turned him down, but the *Overland Monthly*, a Western literary magazine, accepted "To the Man on Trail" for ten dollars. Shortly after that, *Black Cat* accepted his four-thousand-word story "A Thousand Deaths" for forty dollars, provided he would give them permission to cut it in half. London was thrilled. "I told Mr. Umbstaetter he could cut it down two-halves if he'd only send the money along. He did, by return mail."[1]

When "To the Man on Trail" came out in January 1899, London was offered a job at the post office paying forty dollars a month. This was a small fortune compared to his ten cents an hour working in the jute mill. However, based on his two meager successes with writing, he turned the job down. It turned out to be a wise decision. The *Overland Monthly* sale proved to be London's big break. Houghton Mifflin, one of America's most prestigious publishers at that time, took note of his work and offered to publish a collection of his short stories about the Northland. The book, *The Son of the Wolf* (1900), was one of Houghton Mifflin's best-selling books of 1900.[2] On the day it was published, London married Bessie Maddern. Biographer Earle Labor states, "He did not love her but he had genuine affection and respect for her as a friend.... She did not love him, but she enjoyed his natural charm and friendship."[3]

Most of *The Son of the Wolf* stories center on a young half-breed known as the Malemute Kid. The Kid lives by the Northland code, and old-timers and newcomers alike look up to him. The code—a lifestyle of compassion, camaraderie, integrity, selflessness, and situational justice—derives from living through what London terms the White Silence. Some of his most memorable descriptions depict this time of winter:

> Nature has many tricks wherewith she convinces man of his finity—the ceaseless flow of the tides, the fury of the storm, the shock of the earthquake, the long roll of heaven's artillery—but the most tremendous, the most stupefying of all, is the passive phase of the White Silence. All movement ceases, the sky clears, the heavens are as brass; the slightest whisper seems sacrilege, and man becomes timid, affrighted at the sound of his own voice. Sole speck of life journeying across the ghostly

wastes of a dead world, he trembles at his audacity, realizes that his is a maggot's life, nothing more.[4]

Throughout the White Silence, men must rely on each other to survive. They live in small spaces, sharing whatever stock of food and entertainment each has to offer. As with any frontier without a regular police force, the Northland uses frontier justice to keep the peace. London consistently uses this Northland code as a measuring stick of character.

Malemute Kid, who is the "high priest of the code," keeps his head during every crisis and effortlessly applies the code to whatever situation he is in. In "To the Man on Trail," he allows a man who has stolen $40,000 from a gambling house to escape, yet does nothing to aid the Canadian Mounted Police officer who is tracking the thief. His buddies are astounded. Then they learn from the Kid that the man's partner had run off with the money and gambled it away. He was simply getting his money back. He took no more than what he was owed.

Again in "The Men of Forty-Mile," the Kid administers justice to two men ready to fight a duel because of a petty argument about whether the river ice is formed on top of the water or at the bottom of the river. The Kid sets it up so that whoever wins the duel gets hanged for murder. Both men sheepishly withdraw from the duel and justice is served.

In contrast to the Malemute Kid, the two men in "In a Far Country," Carter Weatherbee and Percy Cuthfert, end up killing each other during the White Silence. At first, they perform their tasks of survival with a spirit of camaraderie. That quickly fades as they become petty and suspicious. They end up killing each other over their sugar supply. When measured against the Northland code, they fail miserably.

Jack London, circa 1900

London labels them "Incapables" and holds them up as examples of those who cannot or will not adapt.

Finding His Voice

Success came rapidly after publication of *The Son of the Wolf*. London had found his voice, tapping into the thoughts and feelings of the working class. He studied his markets and knew them well. He proceeded to exploit the market for material gain. He did not hoard his money but used it for his grandiose plans and various adventures that needed funding. Writing became his means to an end. He was known as a generous man and he supported three separate households: his, his mother's, and eventually that of Bessie and his two daughters.

Writing for money highlighted some of the paradoxes in London's socialist philosophies. Even though he was a socialist, he wrote rags-to-riches stories along the lines of Horatio Alger. London himself moved from the working class to the middle class. This rise became problematic for London as a socialist. Later in life, although he still claimed to be a socialist, he lived the life of a rich capitalist. He owned a large ranch complete with hired hands and servants.

paradox

An idea or statement that contains contradictory elements.

After *The Son of the Wolf*, two other short story collections, *The God of His Fathers* (1901) and *Children of the Frost* (1902), were published by Century. *The God of His Fathers* runs in a vein similar to *The Son of the Wolf* except the central character is Sitka Charley, another half-breed with exceptional character.

With *Children of the Frost*, London decided to play with contrasts. He presents a series of Northland stories from the natives' point of view. London is careful to avoid the stereotypes of Indians so often found in stories of the Wild West. Instead, he presents them as loyal, honest, and self-sacrificing. The Indians are often more noble and admirable than the vicious Anglo-Saxon characters in these stories.

All three of these Northland books promote London's ideas on social Darwinism and white superiority. Because this idea was prevalent at the time, both editors and readers tended to overlook this inappropriate strain of thinking. His sympathetic treatment of the natives may have helped, too.

"To Build a Fire" (1910 Version)

Another Klondike story, "To Build a Fire," has become one of America's most reprinted short stories. London actually had two versions of this story published. The 1902 version was published in May in the *Youth's Companion*. In this version, the resourceful main character survives a fall into icy water. In the better-known 1910 version, the protagonist lacks the survival skills he needs and perishes because of his own foolishness. It is this later version that is found in many literature books.

Summary

The story opens as a man with only a dog for a companion sets out for a ten-mile (sixteen-kilometer) trek to a neighboring claim in the Klondike. It is seventy degrees below zero, which means it is one hundred degrees below freezing. But the man does not know this. The unnamed man tests the temperature by spitting in the air. He knows that spit will crackle on the snow at fifty below, but his spit solidifies while

> **protagonist**
>
> The main character in a novel or other piece of writing.

still in the air. He is surprised, and realizes it must be colder than fifty below, but continues on.

The man, a newcomer, has been warned by an old-timer not to go out alone when the temperature drops past fifty degrees below zero. By ignoring this warning, he sets the stage for his inevitable demise. As London writes in the story, "The trouble with him was that he was without imagination. He was quick and alert in the things of life, but only in the things, and not in the significances."[6] He was practical, but did not look for the deeper meanings in life.

Man and beast continue on the trail, with the fact of the cold registering on the man's mind periodically. He is intent on scanning his surroundings for hidden springs of water beneath the ice and the snow, the biggest threat to travelers. He comes across several of these but is able to avoid them. The dog is depressed by the cold, constantly expecting the man to seek shelter or build a fire.

Stopping for lunch at half past noon, the man takes his glove off to retrieve his lunch, which is stored inside his shirt next to his skin to keep it from freezing. Immediately, his exposed fingers become numb. Once again, he registers surprise. The numbness and the ice around his mouth on his beard keep him from being able to eat. He chuckles at himself for forgetting to build a fire to melt the ice from his face and keep his hands warm while he holds his food. He mentally acknowledges that the old-timer from Sulphur Creek spoke the truth about the winters in the Klondike.

The man resumes his trip and then it happens. He breaks through some ice without warning, getting wet from his feet halfway to his knees. To survive, he must stop and build a fire. He knows he must not fail, as the old-timer has warned him. His fire built, he smiles at the old-timer laying down the law about no one going out alone after fifty below zero. The narrator notes, "Well, here he was; he had had the accident; he was alone; and he had saved himself."[7] But he had made a mistake. He built the fire under a spruce tree. As the fire gets going, snow falls from the branches and puts the fire out. He immediately realizes the significance. He "was shocked. It was as though he had just heard his own sentence of death."[8] He must build another fire.

Through much difficulty and using all his matches, he manages to get a second fire going. But his numb body will not cooperate and his shivering hands scatter the burning wood. Both the fire and his hope are extinguished. He briefly considers killing his dog and using the carcass for warmth, but the dog's instincts tell him something is wrong and he avoids the man.

Fear of death overtakes the man and he begins to run along the trail. He collapses several times, finally realizing that he cannot continue. In his practical way, he acknowledges that he will die. As he sits in the snow to die with dignity, he mumbles to the old-timer on Sulphur Creek, "You were right, old hoss; you were right."[9]

Interplay of Literary Devices

London's plotting of this story is very tight. Every sentence in the story moves it toward its conclusion, and every element speaks to the outcome. The story focuses on just one day, and the beginning, middle, and end are clearly identifiable. A man leaves on a journey, filled with arrogance. He suffers a fatal fall through the ice. He admits his mistake before dying with dignity.

The interplay of literary devices is what makes this story so compelling. London sets the atmosphere from the first para-

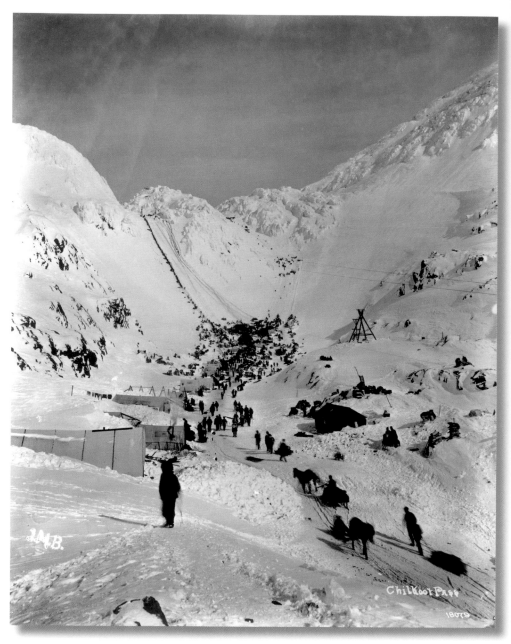

The Klondike, Chilkoot Pass, during the Gold Rush. London's experiences during this time provided the material for stories like "To Build a Fire."

graph using phrases like "exceedingly cold and gray," "dim and little-traveled trail," "intangible pall," and "subtle gloom." The reader can immediately guess that the man is doomed. This imagery, often associated with the White Silence in his other stories, is repeated throughout the story to keep the underlying dread constant.

The technique of flashback shows the main character's progressive realization that he is doomed. The man enters into an ongoing mental dialogue with the old-timer on Sulphur Creek. He recalls the old-timer's advice—initially laughing at it, then realizing its truth.

London's choices in sequencing the events are excellent. He could have started the story with the actual conversation, allowing the reader to meet the wise old man. Instead, London uses the man's internal dialogue with the old timer to show his slow but sure acceptance of the truth: no one should travel alone once the temperature drops to fifty degrees below zero.

Comparative Theme: Intellect Versus Instinct

London picks up one of his favorite Klondike themes in this story: the failure of those who lack imagination to survive in a cold and indifferent world. Although the dog is not a main character, London contrasts the dog's instinct with the man's intelligence. London makes the point that instinct is more important for survival than intellect.

Because the man lacks imagination, his concrete observations of his situation are not enough to save him. This is evidenced in his surprise when his spit crackles in the air instead of on the ground, and then again when the cold freezes his hands as he tries to eat without first building a fire. His mere observations have not alerted him to the seriousness of his situation. What was merely surprise before turns into shock when snow falls on his fire, then to terror when his second fire dies, signaling his imminent demise. Once the facts are clear, the man turns back upon his practical side. He simply sits down to die, admitting his failure.

More Stories

Two other books were published during 1902. One was yet another Northland story, *A Daughter of the Snows*. This was London's first novel and it was not very good. Even London did not like it, realizing "I squandered into it enough stuff for a dozen novels."[10] McClure's, the publisher who promised to publish anything London wrote for them, did not think it was very good, either. McClure's kept its word by passing it off to the publisher J.P. Lippincott. The other book published in 1902 was a collection of juvenile stories based on London's adventures on San Francisco Bay titled *Tales of the Fish Patrol*.

During the flurry of publishing activity in 1902, London's marriage began to show signs of stress. Even so, London wrote his most famous novel, *The Call of the Wild*, during this time. Although his marriage was failing, his career was about to take off.

FIRST MAJOR SUCCESS: THE CALL OF THE WILD

*T*he *Call of the Wild* was a surprise hit, even to the publisher. First serialized in the *Saturday Evening Post*, it sold out its first ten thousand copies in the first day.[1] Critics compared London to Rudyard Kipling, Bret Harte, and Stephen Crane. Although the publisher's special promotion of the book played a part in its success, the book's content had obviously hit a nerve with the American people and would soon touch the imaginations of an international audience.

By this time in his career, London had a working relationship with George Brett of Macmillan Publishing. Macmillan had already published three of London's books, none of which sold very well. Instead of the usual royalties contract, Brett offered to buy *The Call of the Wild* for a one-time payment of $2,000. In exchange, he would be able to print the book immediately and then promote the book with special bindings, illustrations, and advertising. Otherwise, it would be a couple of years before the book would be printed, with royalties coming even later than that. London's earlier books combined had not even earned him $1,000. Weighing the option of a badly needed $2,000 now or waiting a couple of years for an undetermined amount of money, London chose the flat fee for the book.

With the advantage of hindsight, biographer Earle Labor observes, "*The Call of the Wild* was an immediate bestseller, enthusiastically received by reviewers and readers alike. It has remained in print since its first day of publication and has appeared in countless editions in the United States and abroad."[2] Although the book would have eventually made more than $100,000 in royalties for London, he never regretted his decision to accept only $2,000. London understood the value of what had occurred. He knew there was no price tag for what he eventually gained from Brett's marketing arrangement. From this point forward, London was able to demand top dollar for all of his writing.

Stages of the Mythical Hero

The Call of the Wild is divided into seven chapters. Detailing the life of a dog, Buck, these chapters can be divided into sections related to the stages of the mythical hero: a call to adventure, departure, initiation, transformation, and return. Buck's development clearly follows these stages as he goes from being the household pet of a California judge to legendary ghost dog in the frozen Northland.

Chapter 1—Into the Primitive

The story takes place in the early days of the Yukon Gold Rush of 1898. Buck, a St. Bernard and Scotch shepherd mix, leads a comfortable life on the estate of Judge Miller in California. One of the judge's servants steals Buck and sells him to a dog trader. Buck is sent to the Yukon Territory for use as a sled dog.

Abused on his train trip, Buck has turned into a red-eyed, vicious animal by the time he arrives in Seattle. His next master, for a short while, is a man in a red sweater with a club. This man repeatedly fends off Buck's attacks through use of the club. Thus, Buck learns the first lesson of primitive existence: The law of the club, that "a man with a club is a lawgiver, a master to be obeyed, but not necessarily conciliated."[3]

Thoroughly subdued, Buck is sold to a Frenchman, Perrault, and is taken aboard ship to head even farther north. Perrault works carrying dispatches for the Canadian government. On board ship, Buck meets other dogs that will be on Perrault's dogsled team: Curly, Dave, and Spitzbergen (Spitz for short). At their first meal, Spitz steals a bone from Buck's meal, creating an immediate tension between the two dogs. The ship docks and the dogs are brought out into the cold.

Chapter 2—The Law of Club and Fang

Buck's first impressions of the port town of Dyea involve fear, savagery, and confusion. Buck's second lesson comes when a husky attacks Curly as she tries to be friendly. When Curly hits the ground, a group of huskies converge on her, tearing her to pieces. Buck learns another important lesson of the wild: "No fair play. Once down, that was the end of you."[4]

Buck almost immediately begins his life of toil in the traces, the straps and harnesses used to control the sled dog team. He quickly learns how to work as part of a team and how to survive in the wilderness. He learns what it is to be hungry. His food ration never seems to be enough and when he does not eat fast enough, the other dogs steal his food. He watches the other dogs and learns to steal food, not only from the other dogs but from Perrault's cooking stash as well. This descent marks his move from "the law of love and fellowship" that Buck knew in the Southland to his adaptation to "the law of club and fang" in the primitive North. Buck will be a survivor because he adapts.

Chapter 3—The Dominant Primordial Beast

This chapter describes the inevitable battle when Spitz and Buck fight for leadership. When they finally face off, Buck begins fighting by instinct. Spitz, wiser in the ways of the wild, lets Buck wear himself out with rush after rush. When Buck stumbles, with a pack of sixty dogs surrounding him, he realizes he must keep on his feet, so he changes his tactics. He begins to fight with his intellect. He rushes Spitz and breaks one of Spitz's forelegs. Again, he rushes and breaks the other. One last hit and Spitz is on the ground. With the pack moving in, "Buck stood and looked on, the successful champion, the dominant primordial beast who had made his kill and found it good."[5]

Chapter 4—Who Has Won to Mastership

The next morning, Francois and Perrault cannot find Spitz but deduce from Buck's wounds what has happened. Buck takes leadership of the team and proves himself worthy. When they return to Skaguay, the two men are sent on another assignment and the team is turned over to other drivers who work the mail run. These new drivers are fair, but the dogs grow weary. At night, Buck lies by the fire and dreams of the warm Southland and all that he knew there, as in a distant memory. He also dreams of a squat, hairy man tending a fire, an even more distant memory of ancestors long gone. Buck's dreams throughout the story signal how far he is along the path to the primitive.

Chapter 5—The Toil of Trace and Trail

Upon their return to Skaguay, the dogs are too exhausted to be of much use for the mail runs. They are sold to three Americans: Hal, Charles, and Mercedes. Upon seeing the condition of

Buck fights Spitz in *The Call of the Wild*.

their camp, "tent half-stretched, dishes unwashed, everything in disorder,"[6] Buck knew these people were out of place in the Northland. When it is time to take off, the dogs are unable to move their overloaded and top-heavy sled. Hal decides the dogs are lazy and proceeds to whip them mercilessly.

The trio's incompetence continues throughout the journey. Eventually, the group pulls in to John Thornton's camp. After a short stop, Hal and crew decide to continue on. The usual beating is required to get the team going, but Buck refuses to get up. His instincts warn him of some impending doom so he lies still despite being whipped and beaten. Thornton, who has witnessed the attack, puts a stop to it and angrily frees Buck from the traces. Buck and Thornton watch as the party goes out onto the river, only to break through the ice and disappear beneath the water.

Chapter 6—For the Love of a Man

John Thornton becomes Buck's new master, treating him with love and kindness. As Buck recuperates under his care, Buck comes to love Thornton and becomes his protector and defender. But London points out that "the strain of the primitive, which the Northland had aroused in him, remained alive and active."[7]

Buck continues to dream and starts to identify with "shades of all manner of dogs, half-wolves and wild wolves"[8] that lurk about him in the night. London explains, "Deep in the forest a call was sounding."[9] Buck runs toward the forest to answer the call, but each time love for Thornton brings him back.

Chapter 7—The Sounding of the Call

Eventually, Thornton leaves the settlements and goes deep into the wilderness in search of a fabled, lost gold mine. After a year of wandering, Thornton and his companions find gold and begin to mine it, earning thousands of dollars a day. Buck still dreams of the short-legged hairy man, and he still hears the call in the forest. Buck starts returning to the forest more and more often for longer and longer periods. He becomes "a killer, a thing that preyed, living on the things that lived, unaided, alone, by virtue of his own strength and prowess, surviving triumphantly in a hostile environment where only the strong survive."[10]

One day Buck returns to camp and finds it has been attacked by the local Yeehat Indians. All the men and dogs have been killed. The Yeehats are in the midst of celebrating their success when Buck attacks them. Because of his love for

Prospectors with sled dogs make their way to the Yukon Territory.

Thornton, Buck rages through the group, killing as many as he can. The rest flee "proclaiming as they fled the advent of the Evil Spirit."[11] With Thornton gone, "The last tie was broken. Man and the claims of man no longer bound him."[12] Buck answers the call. He returns to the forest and locates the pack of the wolf he befriended the previous year. Buck is accepted into the pack and runs with them from then on.

Over time, the Yeehats notice that the wolf pack begins to take on some new characteristics. These traits are similar to those of the fierce evil one they had seen in the valley of the miners. This dog gets the blame for many of their misfortunes, including dead Yeehats found in the forest, throats slashed. They begin to tell stories of a great Ghost Dog that runs at the head of the wolf pack. Buck's metamorphosis from civilized pet to legendary leader of the wilds is complete.

Interwoven Themes

London incorporated two of his favorite ideologies in this story. Having read Darwin and Spencer, he believed in the evolution of the physical world and of society. In this story, both environment and society play important parts in determining Buck's behavior and future.

Naturalism, Determinism, and the Dominant Primordial Beast

In naturalistic writing, everything happens in the physical realm and is explainable by observation of physical events. London skillfully uses nature to demonstrate how Buck adapts to his new environment. Functioning in the physical environment of the North requires certain skills. Buck must master these new skills not only to thrive, but to survive. For example, the bitter cold requires that Buck learn how to deal with ice between his toes and how to burrow in the snow for warmth at night. Buck is subject to the laws of physics. The sled must be properly loaded so it can be pulled without tipping over. He must figure out how to dislodge the sled from ice and how to get out of the way of the sled on a downhill run. With each new skill learned, Buck becomes less dependent upon man. Eventually, he is totally self-sufficient.

While Buck progresses in his survival skills, he regresses in his social skills. Buck's environment of masters and other dogs determines how he behaves. This concept that environment alone shapes a person is called determinism. London applies determinism to Buck to justify his moral regression. He uses Buck's interactions with his various masters and with other dogs and wolves to do this.

Buck's progression of experiences contrasts his intellectual and physical mastery with his moral decline. For example, the man with the red sweater is Buck's initiation into the "law of the club." He learns that a man with a club is superior to a dog, and man is no longer to be trusted. Buck learns the "law of fang" by watching other dogs devour Curly. This, too, puts him on his guard. These experiences awaken his instinct.

As Buck works for Perrault and Francois, he builds stamina and strength as he toils for hours on end, day after day. He begins to master the relationships within the team. When a dog steals his meat, he studies their methods and becomes the best thief in the camp so that even Perrault does not suspect him. But he learns the most from Spitz. Spitz has instinct and cunning. As the two interact, Spitz is actually training Buck to be the leader. By the end of his stay with Perrault and Francois, Buck has become master of his society. He is superior in both cunning and physical strength.

The unhappy trio that buys Buck provides a nice contrast between those who cannot adapt to the environment and those who can. Their inability or refusal to adapt leads to death. Buck adapts quickly and completely, gaining superiority. Thornton serves a slightly different purpose. Buck's loving response to Thornton proves that even after Buck has completely regressed from his civilized life, he can be reclaimed by love.

London drives home his point on determinism in the last chapter. Buck returns each year to the place where Thornton was killed and pays him homage. Buck's response to love is love. On the other hand, he continues to attack Yeehat hunters year after year. His response to violence is violence.

Buck masters three areas to prove his right to be the dominant primordial beast. First, he masters nature. He learns to live with hunger when there is no food, then to hunt for his own food in the wild. Second, he demonstrates mastery over his own kind. Not only does he kill the dominant Spitz, he takes Spitz's job as leader and outperforms him. He masters all other dogs, whether those on the team or any dog that threatens Thornton.

Lastly, Buck masters mankind. Once Buck is received into the hands of the dog traders, he feels fear for the first time. He learns to fear a man with a club when he meets the man in the red sweater. He develops cautious relationships with each new owner, respecting some and despising others. London makes clear that even though Buck learns to love Thornton, he still retains his hard-earned wilderness instincts. Buck finally masters mankind in the end when he meets the Yeehats in the valley of the miners. Even though the Indians have weapons, his love for Thornton enables him to surmount their advantage. In his rage, Buck becomes fearless and kills even humans.

Anthropomorphism and Primal Needs

By using anthropomorphism, London is able to demonstrate his theories of socialization to good effect. Buck's "de-evolution" into stealing and killing is far less shocking when viewed within the animal kingdom. Yet it only takes a small mental leap to apply the process to humans. One way London accomplishes this feat convincingly is by presenting the story from the dog's point of view. He uses "dog psychology,"[13] presenting the story by inferring the way a dog would think and act. He does this primarily through identifiable human emotions. Buck experiences jealousy and revenge toward Spitz. He demonstrates loyalty, love, and devotion for Thornton. He even shows patience in stalking a moose. Buck's emotions make the transition easier from dog story to human allegory.

> **anthropomorphism**
>
> The act of bestowing animals with human traits.

A second technique of London's is to use basic needs to drive the changes in Buck. For example, hunger often drives Buck's regression. He first learns to steal through hunger. Hunger sharpens his instincts. Hunger fuels his bloodlust. Because hunger is a universal experience, the reader can rationalize or even excuse the regression—especially when Buck's hunger borders on starvation.

The Hero's Journey in Five Stages

Buck's journey from civilization to the primitive follows the typical pattern of the mythical hero. The five general stages of development are a call to adventure, separation, initiation, transformation, and return.[14] As Buck moves through these stages, his moral development regresses while his instincts

57

increase. His very survival depends upon denying his moral training.

The discovery of gold in the Yukon, though it does not involve Buck directly, serves as his call to adventure. Buck's separation occurs when he is taken from Judge Miller's ranch in California and transported to the North. Up to this point, Buck has learned to trust the people in his life. He has had no reason to develop his instincts. From this point of separation, Buck's fears begin to develop and become an integral part of his ability to survive.

Initiation occurs immediately afterward with two major incidents, the law of the club—learned at the hand of the man with the red sweater; and the law of fang—learned as he watches Curly brutalized and killed by a pack of dogs. The initiation flows into a series of tests, demonstrating Buck's ability to adapt to his new environment, combining his civilized intellect and his primitive instincts.

allegory

A story that contains symbols and hidden meanings.

During the hero cycle, a benevolent helper typically aids the hero during his transformation. In Buck's case, his early helpers are Perrault and Francois. They protect him from Spitz as he adapts to life in the wilderness. Once Buck develops his primordial skills, Thornton serves as his escort deep into the wilderness.

In a typical hero story, the hero returns to his point of origin, now stronger and equipped to benefit his fellow man. In *The Call of the Wild*, Buck's return is not to civilization, but to his more primitive, ancestral beginnings as a wild animal. London uses this twist on the hero's return to the primitive instead of the civilized as a nod to Darwin's theories.

London's Desire for Change

In the same year that *The Call of the Wild* was published, 1903, London published eighteen stories and essays, and two more books, and he finished writing *The Sea-Wolf.* He had grown tired of the public's requests for more stories of the Northland and struck out in various directions. Even before *The Call of the Wild* came out, London began experimenting with different types of writing.

Pieces of the World 5

London's kaleidoscope encompasses both fiction and non-fiction, including science fiction, children stories, socialist commentary/propaganda, short stories, and news reporting. Just before *The Call of the Wild* came out, he went international. Partly to escape his failing marriage but mostly to cover his $3,000 of debt, he pursued the job of foreign news correspondent. He accepted a job from the American Press Association to cover the end of the Boer Wars in South Africa. On his way, he stopped in New York to see George Brett. While there, he contracted with Macmillan to write a book on the condition of slums in London's East End during his layover in England. This extra writing gig turned out to London's advantage because his series on the Boer Wars was cancelled and his ticket to England was already paid for.

In England

The title of London's book, *The People of The Abyss*, came from H.G. Wells's term for the urban poor.[1] London arrived in England, disguised himself as a newly arrived down-and-out American sailor, and went to live alongside the people he was reporting on. He experienced the horrors of urban civilization first-hand and reported what he saw. His book was padded with charts and statistics from other sources, but the narrative sections reveal London's outrage at the living conditions of what was then the capitalist center of the Western world: "If this is the best that civilization can do for the human, then give us howling and naked savagery. Far better to be a people of the wilderness and desert, of the cave and the squatting place, than to be a people of the machine and of the Abyss."[2]

London's reference to the wilderness puts his indignation in perspective. After witnessing the physical hardship of the natural environment in the Northland, he decided that man-made hardship created by industrialization was far worse. It fueled the fire of his socialism, moving him from passive protestor to revolutionary. Biographer Labor states, "What affected him most deeply was the hopeless plight of the very old and the inevitable doom of the very young."[3] There

Children play in London's East End at the turn of the twentieth century. London's book *The People of the Abyss* exposed the deplorable conditions he witnessed during the time he spent in these slums.

was no social net for the old; they lived on the streets if they had no family. Seventy five percent of the children would die before age five.[4]

These feelings were probably intensified by London's own narrow escape from the Social Pit, as evidenced in his article "How I Became a Socialist." Written just after his return from England, it reveals his deep-seated fear of falling back into the pit. This article indicates a schism in London's thinking that eventually led him to resign from the Socialist Party just months before his death. Socialists generally identified with the working class and tried to improve their lives. London, on the other hand, feared the working class life and wanted to escape from it.[5] He never overcame this fear, as evidenced in his California novels written toward the end of his career. In *The Valley of the Moon*, the main characters reject their lower-class existence in the city and go in search of an agrarian dream. These characters articulate in London's fiction what he only hints at in his article about becoming a socialist.

The People of The Abyss became very popular at home in the United States. Surprisingly, the book sold almost twenty million copies there, making it quite profitable. In England, the reception was cool. Jack London had revealed the dirty part of industrialization in that country, and it was not taken kindly.[6] And although the book was not a socialist treatise on the poor, it brought London to the forefront of the socialist movement.

A Love Dilemma

Another of London's early attempts to draw away from the Northland stories was coauthored with his friend and love interest Anna Strunsky. London had met Strunsky back in 1899 at some of the socialist meetings he attended. London was attracted to Strunsky but had suddenly decided to marry Bessie Maddern, a woman who fit his ideal for a mother for his desired Anglo-Saxon progeny.

After his marriage, London continued his friendship with Strunsky. Anna was a materialist intellectually but an idealist at heart. She could not decide whether it was better to marry for practical reasons or for reasons of the heart. London proposed that they settle the matter through a series of letters, with him taking the side of logic and science, and with her taking the side of the romantic idealist. The result was a series of letters collected in a book called *The Kempton-Wace Letters*. When London stopped by New York on his way to England, Brett agreed to publish the letters using pseudonyms so as not to distract from the upcoming marketing push for *The Call of the Wild*.

In the letters, Strunsky, using the pseudonym Dane Kempton, tries to convince the younger Wace that romantic love is not only necessary for marriage, but also desirable. London, writing as Herbert Wace, masterfully presents his arguments for foregoing romance for the sake of science. Wace's arguments support London's belief that the best way to produce a superior race is through selective breeding.

Ironically, London had chosen his first wife, Bessie, based on this ideal. While he was writing this book, his own marriage was falling apart. His disillusionment with his scientific ideal became evident when he allowed the Kempton character's ideas to win out in the book. London's experiment with marrying for breeding purposes was a failure.

In Japan

London twice took on the job of war correspondent. The first time, in 1904, he accepted a job from the Hearst Syndicate to report on the Russo-Japanese War. The Japanese and Russians were fighting for control of Manchuria. London arrived in Tokyo, only to find that the journalists were idle, waiting for permission from the Japanese government to go to the front to report on the war.

London, forever the adventurer and tired of waiting, set out on his own for Manchuria via Korea. Upon landing in Korea, he was arrested for being a Russian spy. After convincing the local officials that he was just an American journalist, he was let go. He had two more arrests, the second of which amounted to an international incident. Richard Harding Davis, a famous American journalist, intervened on London's behalf by wiring President Roosevelt about the problem. Roosevelt contacted the Japanese and London was released, with the stipulation that he return home immediately. He complied.

Because the Japanese government hindered the efforts of all reporters, London's war coverage was minimal. He witnessed one battle between the Russians and Japanese. Most of his stories covered his own experiences, detailing his exploits and the condition of the two armies he observed. London had no love for the Japanese. In his reporting, London sided with the Russians. He was very much against the so-called "yellow peril" of the oriental races. (At the time, there was a prevalent fear that Chinese and Japanese immigration would lower the value of the American worker.) He believed that the Japanese should be subjugated to the Russians.

Although he admired their military discipline, London did not appreciate Japan's culture. His tendency toward impulsive action clashed with the Japanese culture of subtlety and pausing to ponder the significance of actions.

When he returned to the United States, London voiced his opinions about his experiences in his socialist meetings.

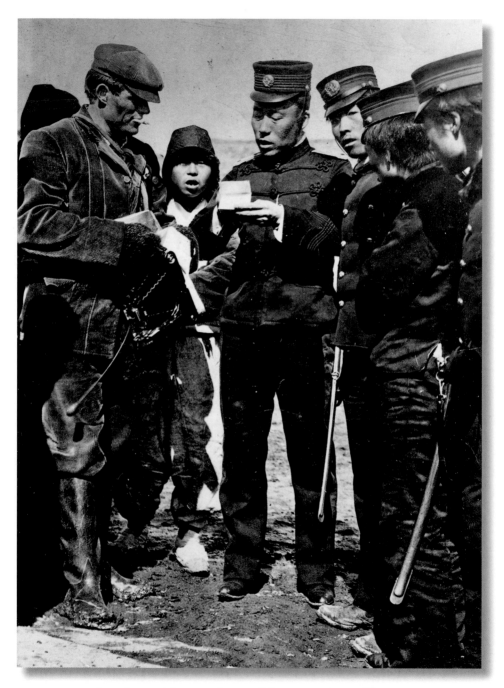

London with members of the Japanese military

His comrades were flabbergasted that he would lambaste the Japanese race as a whole. The socialists were interested in the working class, regardless of race. London's comments, which amounted to racial prejudice, revealed a darker side to the man. When his comrades tried to point out his un-socialist thinking he responded with, "I am first of all a white man and only then a socialist!"[8] Because many of his views were

IN MEXICO

Again in 1914, London took on the job of correspondent, this time during the Mexican Revolution. He worked for *Collier's* for $1,400 a week. In 1910, at the beginning of the conflict, London was against the United States' intervention in the conflict. His short story "The Mexican" is a sympathetic portrait of a Mexican boxer who bests his gringo opponent, using the prize money to buy arms for the revolution.

By the time London went to Mexico in 1914, his attitude had changed dramatically. For example, he now sided with US intervention, which was led by capitalists wanting to exploit the oil fields of Mexico. Second, he no longer spouted the rhetoric of socialism. He spoke out against the common laborer—the very people socialists supported. Living the bourgeois life of riches and travel and owning the ranch made him into a practicing capitalist, even if he still claimed socialist leanings. His articles from this adventure served to discredit him among socialists, journalists, and the general public.[7]

As in the Klondike and the South Seas, London had to cut his adventure short because of health problems. London left the war zone because of an acute attack of dysentery.

inconsistent with those of the socialist movement, some began to consider him a liability to the cause even though he still received invitations to speak at socialist events.

Back Home

In the midst of his work as a war correspondent, London's personal life was in chaos. Upon his return from covering the Russo-Japanese War in 1904, Bessie filed for divorce, claiming extreme cruelty. She strongly suspected London was having an affair. She named Anna Strunsky as his love interest in the divorce papers because of their close association in writing *The Kempton–Wace Letters*. The media got hold of this information and reported it. Anna Strunsky publicly declared she was not involved with London, even though he had proposed marriage to her before he left for England. Bessie confided her troubles to Charmian Kitteredge, the woman who, ironically, should have been named in the divorce papers. London and Kitteredge had kept their affair secret even from their closest friends. When Bessie found out the truth, she never forgave Charmian for pretending concern over Jack's straying.

London's next novel, *The Sea-Wolf*, gives clues about his involvement with and appreciation for Charmian. The sole female character shows up halfway through the story, about the same time London became involved with Charmian. The love story in the book reflects his feelings for her at that time. He now obviously believed wholeheartedly in Dane Kempton's point of view about love.

A Story of Redemption: The Sea-Wolf

With *The Sea-Wolf* (1904), the kaleidoscope turned back to London's earlier days. He called on his experience aboard the *Sophia Sutherland* when he was seventeen. As one biographer notes about his experiences at the time, "He had, however, been highly attuned to life aboard the ship, and would later cull these memories for financial profit well beyond his imagining at this point."[1] To refamiliarize himself with sea life, London took his small sailboat, the *Spray*, and sailed around his old haunts. George Brett thought the timing for a sea story was very good because there were not very many out in the marketplace at that time.

Summary

Humphrey Van Weyden, Dean of American Letters, is on a ferryboat in San Francisco Bay when it capsizes in a collision in the fog. Van Weyden passes out during the rescue effort and begins floating out to sea. A sealing schooner, captained by the nefarious Wolf Larsen, picks him up. Larsen is a brutal sea captain, running a ship that functions as a miniature society where might is right and life has no value.

Van Weyden tries to negotiate a return to San Francisco, but Larsen happens to be one man short on his boat and decides to keep Van Weyden aboard the *Ghost* on a whim. He determines that Van Weyden has stood "on dead men's legs"[2] for too long, referring to his being a gentleman and living solely off his inheritance. Larsen wants to see him work for a living. He believes he is doing Van Weyden a favor by helping him become a man. Humphrey Van Weyden, reduced to the name Hump, is assigned the position of cabin boy. From his newly lowered social vantage point, Hump both witnesses and experiences the brutality that runs rampant on the ship. In this microcosm of society on the sea, evil for evil is the maxim.

Larsen is an enigma to Hump. One day while cleaning Larsen's stateroom, Hump finds a library consisting of Shakespeare, Poe, and Darwin, among others. Hump cannot immediately reconcile the brutal lord of the ship with the

The San Francisco waterfront around 1900. Schooners like the ones shown here are featured in *The Sea-Wolf*.

JACK LONDON'S PHILOSOPHY

Like the character Van Weyden in *The Sea-Wolf*, London was a deep thinker, always trying to figure out life. His published writing and personal letters are filled with quotable insights. Quotes like these have provided inspiration to readers and fans for over one hundred years.

On life:

- The proper function of man is to live, not to exist. I shall not waste my days in trying to prolong them. I shall use my time.

- Life is not a matter of holding good cards, but sometimes, playing a poor hand well.

- And how have I lived? Frankly and openly, though crudely. I have not been afraid of life. I have not shrunk from it. I have taken it for what it was at its own valuation. And I have not been ashamed of it. Just as it was, it was mine.

- The three great things are: good health; work; and a philosophy of life. I may add, nay, must add, a fourth— sincerity. Without this, the other three are without avail; with it you may cleave to greatness and sit among the giants.[3]

On writing:

- Merely because you have got something to say that may be of interest to others does not free you from making all due effort to express that something in the best possible medium and form.[4]

- Advice to Writers: Don't dash off a six-thousand-word story before breakfast. Don't write too much. Concentrate your sweat on one story, rather than dissipate it over a dozen. Don't loaf and invite inspiration; light out after it with a club, and if you don't get it you will none the less get something that looks remarkably like it.[5]

learned volumes he finds. Just before reaching the seal hunting grounds, Larsen begins to experience severe headaches, causing him to retreat to his stateroom for days at a time. When they reach the seal hunting grounds, they encounter Wolf's brother, Death Larsen. The Larsen brothers are similar in all things except one. Death Larsen is barely literate. He has not widened his world through his mind. He functions only on instinct and will.

Various members of the *Ghost's* crew try to escape the ship while out seal hunting, only to be caught and punished severely. One day while out looking for two seamen who ran off during a heavy fog, the *Ghost* comes across a boat with five people in it—four men and a woman. The woman is none other than Maud Brewster, an American poet known by name to Van Weyden, on her way to Japan to recover her health. Van Weyden quickly falls in love with her, as does Larsen.

Tension grows and distrust mounts as the sole woman onboard ship attracts the ship's captain and Hump, now the ship's first mate. Van Weyden's distrust in Larsen proves well-founded when he awakens one night to find Larsen attacking Maud. He quickly intervenes, knowing that this act could be his last. In the middle of the scuffle, Larsen has one of his headache attacks and can no longer fight. Van Weyden helps him into bed, then he and Maud escape on a well-equipped sealing boat. Through cold, rain, and wind, they labor on through the sea until they land on a small, uncharted island.

Living on the island, they resign themselves to a stay of months, possibly even years, while they wait for rescue. They spend weeks building a shelter (with two separate rooms for propriety's sake for the Victorian audience) and stocking it with wood and food for the winter. Throughout this time, they grow in mutual respect for each other. Van Weyden bears the fruit of his newfound masculinity and Maud is an invaluable help to Van Weyden, helping with chores he could never do alone.

Their romantic interlude is interrupted the morning they find the *Ghost* floating in the cove they call home. Van Weyden investigates and finds that the ship has been abandoned, all except for Wolf Larsen. The crew has gone over to Death Larsen's ship, but not before damaging the masts and sails. In addition, Wolf Larsen's headaches have gotten so bad that he is now blind and in pain much of the time.

Van Weyden decides to repair the *Ghost* and sail it back to waters where they are likely to meet other boats. Upon finishing the repairs, Van Weyden and Maud sail off into the sunset. Larsen suffers another series of strokes and dies shortly after they set sail.

They give him a burial at sea just as they sight another boat to rescue them. The story ends with Maud calling Van Weyden her man, and Van Weyden calling Maud "his one small woman."[6]

Thematic Interplay of Might Versus Right

There are several themes working throughout this story. The most obvious theme is the one espoused by Larsen: might is right. Larsen feels justified in doing what he does simply because he is the strongest. Wrapped within this theme of might is right is the idea that there is no inherent value to life. This theme can be traced to London's view of Darwinism. Darwinism implies that individual lives are not as important as propagation of the species; therefore life only has value as far as it can make the species stronger. The death of weak individuals is not only logical but is expected and even desirable.

London writes *The Sea-Wolf* at Wake Robin Lodge.

Larsen obviously holds to this same view, but he cannot reconcile it with the will to live. In Larsen's view, life is only valuable to the person living it. He declares that even though a life is worthless, the will to live remains strong. Here, London uses German philosopher Nietzsche's idea of the will to power and plays it against the instinctual will to live. However, London was not really true to Nietzsche's ideas because "London, like other Americans, mangled Nietzsche, who insisted man must conquer the inner beast in his search for power, not unleash its reckless and destructive powers."[7] Larsen uses his will to power destructively. For example, Larsen, in his typically sadistic way, nearly chokes Van Weyden to death. When Van Weyden resists, Larsen proves that Van Weyden's will to live is stronger than his willingness to die.

Another minor theme is that of courage. Throughout the story, Van Weyden finds himself growing in courage. His soft life as a scholar has given him no opportunity to develop courage. In contrast, each encounter on board the *Ghost* gives him the chance to grow stronger—both physically and mentally. Van Weyden's greatest revelation comes when he sees that Wolf Larsen is truly fearless. Van Weyden realizes that because Larsen has no fears, he has no true courage. London uses this realization to separate the two men: Larsen is one-dimensional in his power; he is all about brute strength. Van Weyden, on the other hand, tempers his courage with idealism. Van Weyden has become a man while Larsen remains like an animal.

Plot Twist: From Adventure to Romance

London's handling of the plot takes some surprising turns. He starts out creating what has been called one of American literature's most memorable characters in Wolf Larsen, but then introduces a main character halfway through the book. At that point, he turns a story of high adventure into a Victorian romance. Many critics at the time thought the introduction of Maud Brewster at the halfway point was bad plotting. However, London stated that he used the presence of the woman to prove Van Weyden's newly acquired manhood. Larsen was the foil against which he earned his manhood while Maud was the foil against which he proved it.

Modern critics have delved deeper and examined the roles of male and female in this work. In the beginning Van Weyden is described as effeminate. He has to earn his manhood on the high seas. Maud is the era's New Woman. Although frail, she does a man's work when they escape, but she remains completely feminine. By the end of the story, both Van Weyden and Maud have achieved a sort of androgyny.[5] They are clearly male and female, but both exhibit characteristics of the opposite sex. Viewed in light of London's recent affair with Charmian, this showed his appreciation for her similar characteristics. At the same time, he challenged society's view of the masculine and feminine.

A Classic Initiation Story

The Sea-Wolf follows one of London's favorite themes—the initiation story. Van Weyden's dunking in the bay serves as his baptism and rebirth into his new life aboard the *Ghost*. The novel is structured so that Larsen starts out strong and declines throughout the story while Van Weyden begins weak and becomes strong.[6] As the story progresses, Larsen begins to decline because of his headaches and neurological problems, the unsuccessful mutiny of the crew,

> **foil**
>
> A character whose purpose is to serve as a contrast to another.

and the appearance of his brother, Death Larsen, who is more evil and brutal than he is.

While Larsen is declining in power and strength, Van Weyden is learning how to be a man in a man's world. He learns how to work for a living, how to defend himself against evil, and how to overcome his fears. The crossover point occurs when Larsen accosts Maud Brewster and Van Weyden comes to her defense. From that point forward, Van Weyden gains the superior position.

London with his second wife, Charmian

This interplay between duality and reversal is yet another of London's favorite techniques. In *The Sea-Wolf*, London may have tried to cram too much into a single story. He was much more successful with duality and reversal when he used two completely different stories to make his points, such as in *The Call of the Wild* and *White Fang*.

London's Divorce and Remarriage

London rushed *The Sea-Wolf* to completion by the end of 1903. He also separated from Bessie at this time. It took two years for his divorce to become final. On November 19, 1905, he married his new love, Charmian Kitteredge, while on a tour of the United States giving talks on socialism. Marrying her so abruptly after his divorce was shocking and offensive to many people. For a time, it adversely affected his career and public image.

The Sea-Wolf was London's second most popular book until 1906, when *White Fang* surpassed it in popularity and sales. As with *The Call of the Wild*, London used animals to tell his story.

7
APPEASING HIS READERS: WHITE FANG

Relying on past experiences again, London's kaleidoscope shifts back to the Northland. Even though his writing was still popular, his readers wanted more stories from the Northland. London obliged by working on a project he conceived when writing *The Call of the Wild*. Back in 1902, London told George Brett, "I'm going to give the evolution, the civilization of a dog— development of domesticity, faithfulness, love, morality."[1] *White Fang* was a deliberate attempt by London to reverse the process he described in *The Call of the Wild*. Although *White Fang* was never as popular as *The Call of the Wild*, the public received it well. The book sold enough copies to make a healthy profit for Macmillan.

Summary

Part 1—The Wild

Two men, Bill and Henry, are being tracked by a pack of hungry wolves as they travel through the frozen Northland. There is a she-wolf among the pack that is half dog. Over time, she lures the men's sled dogs away, until Bill decides to go after her with a shotgun. Henry stays back, watching and listening to the pursuit. He hears three shots, a cry, and then no more. The wolves have devoured Bill and the last of the dogs.

Henry spends the night alone, staying awake near the fire to keep the wolves at bay. Each night thereafter, the wolves become more desperate, closing in on Henry in spite of the fire. He finally ends up building a circle of fire around himself to keep the wolves away. As that fire burns out, the wolves approach. He sits in the circle of dying flames and goes to sleep, knowing that the wolves have won. Instead, he awakens to silence. The appearance of a group of men has scared the wolves away.

Part 2—Born of the Wild

The she-wolf mates with one of the pack leaders, giving birth to a litter of five pups. A time of famine comes and all the pups die except one. This one has a wolf's coloring, a dog's intelligence, and the stamina of a strong, wild wolf. The pup's first lesson is on hunting. He quickly learns, "The aim of life was meat . . . There were the eaters and the eaten. The law was: EAT OR BE EATEN."[2]

One day, in the midst of the famine, a lynx invades their lair and attacks the mother. When the lynx brings the mother down, the pup joins the attack and the two of them kill the lynx. Although the mother is seriously wounded, she recovers and they begin to go out together to hunt for food.

Part 3—The Gods of the Wild

One day near the lair, the pup comes across a new type of living thing—a "man-god." The pup goes to live in the Indian camp with the one named Gray Beaver, who names the pup White Fang. He learns the laws of living with humans and with those of his own kind. Through several beatings, each more severe than the last, he learns that his man-god, Gray Beaver, is to be obeyed at all times. The other pups take the lead of Lip-Lip, the dominant pup, and torment White Fang. White Fang becomes a ferocious fighter and a loner. Because of this

Wild dogs from *White Fang* circle the fire.

shunning, "he never knew a moment's security. The tooth of every dog was against him, and the hand of every man."[3]

Part 4—The Superior Gods

During the early part of the Klondike gold rush, Gray Beaver goes into the town of Dawson to trade his furs. White Fang, with his distinctive wolf coloring, attracts a lot of attention. One onlooker, Beauty Smith, decides he must own White Fang. Since he knows "the ways of Indians,"[4] he befriends Gray Beaver, giving him a gift of whiskey, then sells him bottle after bottle. Soon, Gray Beaver is indebted to Smith and hands over White Fang.

Beauty Smith is an evil man filled with evil ways. Smith beats White Fang, leaves him tied up all day, and eventually cages him. Smith puts him on public display where people point at him and poke him with sticks to see his vicious reaction. White Fang learns hostility and hatred. Smith plans to make money off White Fang by entering him into dogfights.

White Fang, now known as "The Fighting Wolf," bests all dogs he fights. He even fights two dogs at once, and a lynx at another time. He beats them all until the day he is faced with a bulldog. They enter into a fight to the death. This fight is almost at an end when Weedon Scott, a mining expert from a nearby claim, splits the dogs apart and buys an all-but-dead White Fang to save him from Smith. White Fang has never known love and takes a while to warm up to Scott. In the end, love prevails and White Fang gives his allegiance to Scott.

Part 5—The Tame

The time comes for Weedon Scott to return home to California. Scott takes White Fang home to his estate of his father, who is a judge. White Fang must learn yet another new set of rules for life in the Southland. He learns to tolerate Scott's children, to get along with the dogs on the estate, and to overcome his strong instincts to chase the other animals on the ranch.

One day an escaped convict, Jim Hall, comes to seek revenge on Judge Scott, for sentencing him to prison for a crime he did not commit. As Hall gains the stairway in the entrance hall, White Fang attacks. Man and beast fight it out with gun and fang. By the time Scott and his father make it downstairs, Hall is dead and White Fang is almost dead. The vet gives White Fang a slim chance of survival. White Fang beats the odds and goes on to father a litter of pups.

A Study in Determinism

White Fang functions as a fable, with the moral lesson that society makes the man. London preaches environmental determinism throughout the story, often through direct statements from the narrator. For example, the two reprobates in the story, Beauty Smith and Jim Hall, are both described as shortchanged by nature in their physical make-up and the people around them treat them evilly. Therefore, London asserts, they are not responsible for being the way they are: brutal and unloving toward man and beast. London makes similar statements about White Fang, attributing his changes to those around him.

By using a dog as the main character, London takes the emphasis on environment one step further. Dogs in the real world are subject to their owners. Likewise, White Fang is never free to make his own decisions or create his own reality. His circumstances are dictated by his man-god. Free will—which is nonexistent in the purest form of determinism—is severely limited. He is forced into the role of responder. His character is predicated upon the environment around him, especially the treatment he receives from others. When beaten into submission, he is submissive. When lovingly handled by Scott, he is loving.

Setting as Part of Plot Development

Setting plays a major part in demonstrating the effects of environment on White Fang. In each part of the story, the setting is less wild and more civilized. Initially, White Fang's mother is shown totally in the wild, even though she has obviously had domestication in her life at some point. Part two shows White Fang living in the wilderness and learning to hunt for his food. He is a wild thing learning the laws of the wild—hunting for his own food and fighting his own fights.

Part three moves White Fang into an Indian camp where he learns to live with men and with those of his own kind. In the fourth part, White Fang moves to the town of Dawson, learning how to live with a multitude of men in a closer setting. By part five, White Fang goes to live in the country on Judge Scott's estate. By moving White Fang around so much, London shows the various levels of society the animal must master in order to become civilized.

Reason over Instinct as the Means to Self-Control

Throughout the story, there is a dual conflict going on. Externally, the conflict flares between White Fang and society. He is hated by man and beast alike during his stay in the Indian camp. His instinctive response is to fight back and dominate. But when he does, Gray Beaver beats him into submission. He begins to overcome instinct in order to function in the human world. This sets up the second conflict: White Fang versus himself, or his inner nature. London uses these two conflicts

White Fang at the Indian camp. By entering the Indian camp, the wild animal moves one step closer to civilization.

to highlight the interplay of instinct and intellect during White Fang's domestication.

With each change of setting, White Fang learns more about how to live among men. He learns to assert reason over instinct, displaying a new level of self-control with each change of ownership. With Beauty Smith, his control comes from hatred. By the time he meets Scott, his instinctual fighting response is well under control but he still has one more step to take. He needs to learn to control himself out of love, not fear. The proof of this love comes when White Fang defends the judge's family from attack, even though he suffers near-fatal wounds. With this sacrifice, his metamorphosis is complete.

Comparison of London's Two Dog Stories

In order to achieve his complete reversal of the decivilizing process seen in *The Call of the Wild*, London uses a lot of the same settings and character types. *Call* starts on a California estate, moves to the city, and eventually to deep in the wilds. *White Fang* starts in the wild, moves to the city, then to a country estate in California. Both Buck and White Fang meet inept owners, indifferent owners, and those who show love. Buck's owners escort him from civilization to the wild. White Fang's owners introduce him slowly but surely to civilization.

London chose different genres and underlying philosophies for his two tales. *Call* is a hero story; *White Fang* is a fable. The first tells a tale; the second makes a point. The hero story is told in the context of naturalism; the fable in the context of determinism. Buck reverts to a natural, instinctual existence; White Fang conquers instinct to become civilized.

Both stories emphasize the need to adapt in order to survive. Buck's entry into the rugged wilderness requires the same level of adaptability for survival as White Fang's entry into civilization. Both dogs are shaped by adversity, and their ultimate success depends on fully developing both intellect and instinct.

President Roosevelt Shares an Opinion

White Fang's popularity was helped along when the president, Theodore Roosevelt, read it and called London and other writers "nature fakirs." Nature fakirs falsify the natural world in order to make a point or further an agenda. Roosevelt said he felt compelled to point out the unrealistic representation of animal behavior in London's novel, especially the besting of a wolf by a bulldog. Roosevelt's comments appeared in an article in *Everybody's Magazine.* London responded in *Collier's,* claiming freedom of literary license.

fable

A story with a moral or lesson, often involving animals.

The president was not alone in his criticism. Many experts familiar with wolves decried London's descriptions of interactions between wolves and humans. Wolves are typically terrified of humans and only attack in extreme cases of hunger. However, the reading public either did not notice or did not care. They bought the story as a true representation of animal behavior. London helped perpetuate the still-common myth of the mighty, attacking wolf.

London Leaves the Northland

Just as White Fang made a move from the Northland to southern climes, Jack London did the same in his writing. In real life, he embarked on a world cruise aboard his boat the *Snark.* His first stop was Hawaii. He would then sail on to the South Seas, where a whole new world awaited him.

PIECES OF ADVENTURE ON THE HIGH SEAS: THE CRUISE OF THE SNARK

Twist the kaleidoscope again and you will find another change in London's work. As he traveled and matured, his outlook on life changed. He still tended to promote the underdog, but he changed how he wrote about nature. Instead of nature merely being a strong force hostile to man, it now became chaotic and unpredictable. As the story of his adventures unfolds, this change begins to make sense.

London wrote *The Cruise of the Snark* to make money to pay for his voyage around the world and the continuing work at the ranch. It is filled with slice-of-life stories about the trip and has the feel of a romance novel. London's boat was named after the creature in Lewis Carroll's tale *The Hunting of the Snark: An Agony in Eight Fits.* The story of that ill-fated cruise was but a harbinger of things to come for London's *Snark.* London's cook on the voyage, Martin Johnson, wrote his own book several years later titled *Through the South Seas with Jack London* (1913). His book is quite different from London's. It reads more like a documentary, with personal details from his diary and bits of history thrown in. The two books, when read together, tell a more complete story of London's trip to the South Pacific.

London (*far right*) with his wife and others on board the *Snark*

A Shaky Launch

About four years before the trip began, the Londons had read Joshua Slocum's *Sailing Alone Around the World.* Slocum had made the trip in a thirty-five-foot (ten-meter) boat, taking three years to complete the journey. The Londons began to think about the possibilities of doing the same thing. They soon decided that they could do it together in a 45-foot (13-m) boat. They planned a seven-year voyage that began in San Francisco and went to Hawaii, the South Seas, the Far East, around Africa, to Europe, then back to America, cutting across the continent on various rivers and canals. The boat was designed to sail the high seas and to navigate through rivers so they could explore inland along rivers like the Seine (France) and the Rhine (Germany).

The building of the boat was a catastrophe. The cost, estimated at $7,000 (Slocum's cost him less than $600), went up to $30,000. London could have bought a similar boat for well under $10,000 but he wanted the satisfaction of building it himself. As he explains in the foreword to *The Cruise of the Snark,* "The thing I like most of all is personal achievement—not achievement for the world's applause, but achievement for my own delight. It is the old 'I did it! I did it! With my own hands I did it!'"[1]

In order to pay for the boat and to continue running the ranch in his absence, he contracted with various magazines and book publishers for stories related to the trip. When the *Snark* left the dock in San Francisco, it was barely seaworthy. London decided to sail it to Hawaii and make repairs there—away from the media and his friends, who had been taking bets on his departure date for months beforehand. The Londons and their crew made it in twenty-seven days, although the newspapers had already published accounts stating they were lost at sea.

After several months of repairs, the *Snark* was ready to return to the sea. From Hawaii, it traveled to the South Seas, visiting Tahiti, Typee, the Fiji Islands, and the Solomon Islands. Eventually, the entire crew came down with various tropical diseases. The Londons moved on to Australia to seek medical care. There, London decided to abandon the trip. Although both grieved the loss of their great adventure, Charmian felt the loss most keenly. London said, "In hospital when I broke the news to Charmian that I must go back to California, the tears welled into her eyes. For two days she was wrecked and broken by the knowledge that the happy, happy, voyage was abandoned."[2] Before leaving Australia, London sold the *Snark* for a mere $3,000.

In Hawaii

Although Hawaii did not become a state until 1959, the Hawaiian government had ceded the "Kingdom of Hawaii" to the US government in 1889, giving the American government complete sovereignty over the nation. The islanders were multicultural, with Americans, native islanders, Japanese, and Chinese living there. While repairs were made to the *Snark*, Jack and Charmian toured the islands and were the guests of many of Hawaii's elite. They socialized with dignitaries and commercial barons. They climbed the peaks of Hawaii's volcanoes. But when they spent their Fourth of July on the island of Molokai at a colony for people with leprosy, they ran into resistance from the upper classes.

London wrote several stories featuring Hawaii. One of his most famous is "Koolau the Leper." In this story, a small group of lepers on the island of Kauai has banded together to resist deportation to Molokai and the leper colony. They retreat to a small paradise high in the mountains and take a stand. After many are killed and the rest surrender, Koolau alone remains on the run from the army. He fends them off with his Mauser gun, pulling the trigger with the joint on his thumb—the last digit left that can work the trigger. The army chases him for six weeks, then finally leaves him in peace. Koolau lives another two years, killing those who seek him, but only in self-defense.

LONDON BRINGS SURFING TO CALIFORNIA

When Jack and Charmian London visited Hawaii in 1907, he learned how to surf and, as part of his plan to fund his trip through writing, wrote about his experience. His 4,000-word description of how to surf, how waves form and the wave rider culture appeared in the *Ladies Home Companion* in the October 1907 issue. It is also included in his book *The Cruise of the Snark*.

Beause of several decades of cultural changes, surfing was dying a slow death as the "sport of kings" in the Hawaiian Islands. Jack was recruited to learn how to surf by surfing promoter Alexander Hume Ford. Jack readily took to the sport and wrote about it enthusiastically. Since London's works were widely read in his time, he is credited with reviving the sport of surfing and transporting it to the West Coast.

Ford took advantage of this spotlight on the sport and petitioned to form a club in Hawaii to protect a portion of Waikiki Beach to preserve the island sports of surfing and outrigger canoeing. In 1908, the Outrigger Canoe Club was formed. When London returned to Hawaii in 1915, the club had 1,200 members.

When he senses his life is at its end, he crawls into a thicket to die. He had achieved his goal of dying a free man rather than a prisoner of Molokai. London masterfully paints the poignant scene of Koolau's final moments:

> His eyelids fluttered wearily down and the drip of the rain ceased in his ears. A prolonged trembling set up in his body. This, too, ceased. He half-lifted his head, but it fell back. Then his eyes opened, and did not close. His last thought was of his Mauser, and he pressed it against his chest with his folded, fingerless hands.[3]

Two other short stories, "The Sheriff of Kona" and "Good-bye, Jack" also reveal the plight of the leper in the islands. In his stories, the colony on Molokai is painted as it was in its earliest days—as a last resort prison for people afflicted with leprosy. Yet in his nonfiction book *The Cruise of the Snark*, London paints a picture of the Molokai he saw—a paradise for lepers cast out by society but living happily.

Literary License Leads to Problems

When London reverts to using the earlier conditions of the leper colony in his stories, he is not just adding dramatic tension. He is a making a blatant political statement. Although probably not obvious to the average American reader of the time, it was painfully obvious to the Hawaiian elite who had just entertained the Londons in high fashion.

For example, in "Koolau the Leper," the conflict seems to be man against man, at least on the surface. Digging a little deeper, the conflict is really about man versus society. London makes his political statement in the opening lines spoken by Koolau: "Because we are sick they take away our liberty. We have obeyed the law. We have done no wrong. And yet they would put us in prison."[4] After giving the history of the inva-

Jack and Charmian relax on Waikiki Beach, Hawaii, in 1915.

sion of the white imperialists—making no distinction between the missionaries and the merchants—he goes on to say, "They live like kings in houses of many rooms, with multitudes of servants to care for them. They who had nothing have everything."[5]

Adding insult to injury, London points out through Koolau that the disease they now suffer came from the Chinese slaves, brought there by white imperialists. The inhabitants who once lived peacefully on the islands were now subject to another race and the laws they made. Koolau realizes his stand against the imperialists will not win the war, but it will preserve his personal dignity.

After these stories were published, London's books were removed from bookstores and libraries in Hawaii for a time. London, demonstrating sympathy for the lepers, incited the wrath of the Hawaiian elite who had shown him hospitality. By using leprosy as a "backdrop for the struggle against imperialism,"[6] he portrays the islanders as unsympathetic to both the physical plight of the lepers and the social plight of the native islanders. London heightens the effect by playing on the public's natural fear of leprosy, often giving his characters extreme cases. Not all lepers rotted away to the grotesque figures that he describes.

Whether viewed as entertainment or political statement, London's use of the earlier, squalid conditions of the colony shows his mastery of reading the market, then romanticizing his experiences for his readers. London, as usual when confronted about his stories, pointed out that they were simply works of fiction. He always felt justified using fictional techniques to highlight the problems with the real world around him.

To the Solomons

In London's stories of the North, nature is a fierce foe, but it can be understood by those with imagination and it brings out the best in those who adapt to its harshness. In the South Seas, nature is chaotic and brings out the worst in man. London's negative view of the South Sea Islands was probably the result of the tropical diseases that he and his crew suffered there. These diseases eventually cut short his proposed trip around the world in the *Snark*.

London chose to portray white imperialists at their worst, rotting away under the effects of heat, disease, and alcohol. He chose to portray the Solomon Island natives at their worst, too—cannibals who measured success in the number of heads they collected, especially those of white men. In many of his South Seas stories, human suffering abounds, whether that of the white man or native. When physical health declines, man's morals deteriorate as well. In London's writing, white men in this lowered condition resort to cruelty toward the natives in an exercise of their supremacy. The natives respond with counterattacks and rebellion.

London once again supports the underdog. Even though he accepted Anglo-Saxon superiority as fact, he did not believe in mindless oppression of those conquered. He uses irony to point out the folly of those whose philosophy does include it. A good example of the interplay of oppressed and oppressor is found in his short story "Mauki."

In this story, London creates the character Bunster, a demented white man who delights in cowardly acts of brutality. He acquires a slave, Mauki, who puts up with Bunster's acts of violence, constantly looking for a way to retaliate. Mauki bides his time, and the time finally comes. Bunster falls ill of

95

a fever. Mauki cares for him throughout, but when Bunster is past the fever and still weak, Mauki takes his revenge. He uses a ray skin glove of Bunster's that scrapes the skin off at a single swipe. Bunster has used this glove on many of the islanders, but mainly on Mauki.

Mauki proceeds to skin Bunster alive, leaving him to die. Mauki then goes out to load his boat. London describes the final, grotesque scene: "It was while engaged in this that a hideous, skinless thing came out of the house and ran screaming down the beach till it fell in the sand and mewed and gibbered under the scorching sun. Mauki looked toward it and hesitated. Then he went over and removed the head, which he wrapped in a mat and stowed in the sternlocker of the cutter."[7] London uses irony to illustrate white supremacy gone very wrong. Bunster's moral callousness has been repaid "by having his thick hide removed entirely, and his sadistic head has become the trophy of its principal victim."[8]

Still in the Spotlight

The entire trip of the *Snark* was of great interest to magazines and newspapers. London's lifestyle lent itself to high drama and was therefore newsworthy. This trip was no exception. The media followed it with avid interest. London kept this interest alive by continuing to produce books and by writing stories for magazines that appeared in print as he traveled.

Even on the cruise and in Hawaii, London wrote his one thousand words a day. He had to keep writing to fund his trip and the ranch back home. He completed two novels during this time. One, *The Iron Heel*, was a futuristic tale of a socialist overthrow of the government. It was not much of a success with the public or with socialists. His other novel, *Martin Eden*, was written during the early part of the voyage.

Biographical Bits

Because of London's tendency to romanticize his real-life experiences in his stories, many biographers have taken London's fiction and quoted it as fact. At times, it is hard to tell the difference. London wrote two novels that add depth to his kaleidoscope and reveal much about the man behind the hype. *Martin Eden* (1909), a work of fiction, tells the tale of a seaman who, in three short years, becomes a phenomenally successful writer. It has many autobiographical elements related to London's rise to fame and his rise above the working class. In a twist on taking fiction as real life, critics at the time derided the meteoric rise of the character as unrealistic, but Jack London claimed, "I was Martin Eden."[1] The second book, *John Barleycorn*, is subtitled *Alcoholic Memoirs*, and it details London's life-long struggle with alcohol. This one was mostly accepted at face value as a work of nonfiction.

Meteoric Rise in *Martin Eden*

As the story opens, Martin Eden is entering the home of a middle-class young man he has rescued from a fight on the docks. Although Eden feels very out of place, the man's sister, Ruth, enchants him. The family accepts him in their home and he determines to better himself through education. Ruth, who is falling in love with Eden even though she does not realize it, decides to help Eden in his self-improvement venture. Like Professor Higgins with Eliza Doolittle, Ruth attempts to mold

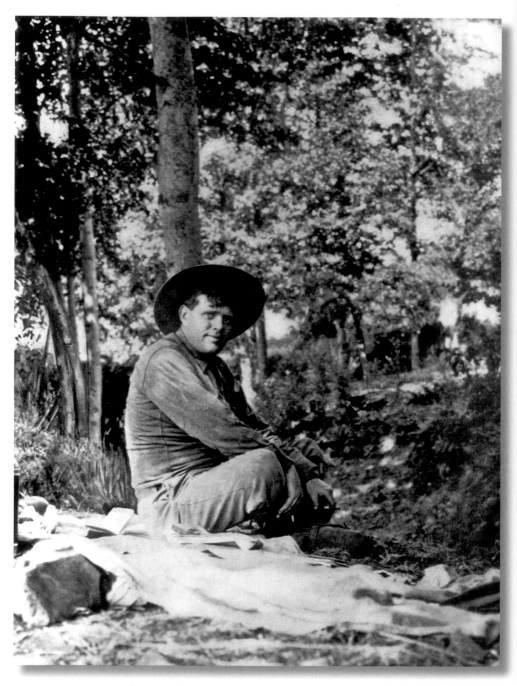

London outdoors with writing materials at hand

Eden into the man that she would like him to be. And like Eliza Doolittle, Martin Eden has feelings and ideas of his own that do not mesh with Ruth's plans.

As Eden begins to show dramatic improvement, Ruth encourages him to find suitable work, even suggesting a place of employment for him. However, Eden wants to become a writer. He forsakes the sea and ignores Ruth's suggestions. He rents a room from a Portuguese woman, becoming the stereo-typical starving artist—literally on the edge of starvation. He allows himself only five hours of sleep a night, and he repeat-edly pawns his belongings to keep writing, then buys them back when he gets paid for his work. Ruth, growing frustrated with his lack of success and refusal to go a more conventional route, rejects him.

During this time in the gutter, Eden meets a man named Brissenden. This gentleman comes and goes, buying dinners occasionally for the starving Eden, and introduces him to the socialist movement in the Bay area. For the first time in his life, Eden has to defend what he believes. He thrives in this intellectually challenging environment, although he never really pursues it apart from Brissenden.

In the meantime, Eden sends out manuscript after manu-script, but most of them are returned. One day, he finally gets a big break. From that point forward, he is never in need of cash and never writes anything new. He simply resends out all the old writing that was originally rejected by the same publishers who are now eager for anything he has to sell.

His success assured, Ruth returns on the eve of an ocean voyage Eden is about to take to escape what his life has become. Ruth asks Eden to forgive her and take her back. Eden refuses. He leaves for his trip, only to slip through the porthole of his stateroom during the voyage to end his misery.

From Working Class to Middle Class

The story functions as a bildungsroman, a novel of the education or personal development of an individual. This education usually happens within the context of a specific social order, while the "student" moves from innocence to (sometimes unhappy) knowledge. Martin Eden goes from a state of intellectual innocence as a working-class seaman to an unhappy knowledge of middle-class success.

In the early part of the novel, Eden's desire to know is fueled by his feelings for Ruth and his ambition. Ruth's rejection of his writing leads to emotional pain. The seemingly random acceptance of his writing leads to disillusionment. Both the fickle love of Ruth and the pinnacle of success—his two trophies for achieving middle-class status—leave him empty. The last lines of the book, spoken as he is drowning, sum up his discovery: "And somewhere at the bottom, he fell into darkness. That much he knew. He had fallen into darkness. And at the instant he knew, he ceased to know."[2] His education is complete.

The critical response to *Martin Eden* was less than enthusiastic. London had attempted the book as a condemnation of individualism. Instead, it appeared that London was promoting it through Eden's actions. The popular response was more positive.

Parallels Between Writer and Character

A bildungsroman often contains autobiographical elements. There are many parallels between London and Eden. The most telling of these is their common view of the social classes. Like London, Eden begins in the lower class. Both long to rise above it; both choose to do so through writing. Both experience a meteoric rise to fame.

Two of the main characters are modeled after people that London knew well. The first, Ruth Morton, is modeled after London's first love Mabel Applegarth. The Applegarth family provided his introduction into middle-class society. Initially, London was impressed by Mabel's beauty and position, but he eventually came to the conclusion that all women (or most of them, anyway) are really the same underneath, whether high born or low born. The other character, Brissenden, closely resembles London's friend, the poet George Sterling. Both are poets, both have socialist leanings, and each has become a sounding board for his literary friend.

> **bildungsroman**
>
> A novel dealing with the education or development of a young protagonist, who then takes his place in society as a mature or knowledgeable adult.

The primary autobiographical merit comes from studying Eden's life and thought processes as he goes through the change from seaman to writer, from the working class to the middle class. For example, Eden pursues his goals with everything that is within him. London, in his lifetime, would often pursue whatever his latest passion was to the end—sometimes a fruitful end and other times an unsuccessful one. His successful pursuits are well documented. But one example of a failed pursuit is his marriage to Bessie Maddern, in which London pursued his theory of marrying for breeding instead of for love.

Another example is his building the *Snark*. His insistence on building it himself led to a barely seaworthy vessel and much unnecessary expense.

In the case of Eden, he pursues his passion until he goes from being an unknown writer to being famous. With fame comes recognition and all the material things he lacked as a starving beginner. Eden struggles with the hypocrisy of the situation. He feels he is still the same—the only thing that has changed is that he has been published.

Unlike *Martin Eden*, Jack London did not treat his celebrity status as emptiness. Instead, he realized that the money his work demanded could be used to fund his dreams of adventure and his plans for his beloved ranch. He claimed he did not like to write. He once told a friend, "I assure you that I do not write because I love the game. I loathe it. . . . The only reason I write is because I am well paid for my labor—that's what I call it—labor."[3] There may be some truth to these statements, especially when put in perspective with his love of fun and adventure. However, it is obvious he realized that writing was what pulled him from the lower class and that he had indeed succeeded in his work.

A Writer's Struggle with *John Barleycorn*

The second autobiographical work, *John Barleycorn* (1913), was written at Charmian's suggestion. It is subtitled *Alcoholic Memoirs* and describes London's struggle with "John Barleycorn," a nickname at that time for hard liquor. The work focuses solely on London's struggles with alcohol, leaving out many details of his life that would naturally fit in an autobiography. For example, much of the debauchery likely associated with London's drinking is left out. Many biographers flag him as a womanizer, but none of this is apparent in this work. As a matter of fact, he presents himself as pure emotionally when it comes to women, leaving out the impurity of the physical that is alluded to several times in *Martin Eden*. Once again, the reason for removing the baser parts of the story is because of the editors' sensitivity to their Victorian audiences. This cleanup work actually helps the book, forcing the focus onto

Jack and Charmian London. Frontispiece to *John Barleycorn*.

London and his ongoing dialogue with John Barleycorn rather than on the side effects of alcohol.

A Constant Companion

According to the book, Jack London's first association with alcohol was at five years old. He was carrying a bucket of beer to his stepfather and stopped to drink some on the way. From this first taste of alcohol, he claims to hate the taste of the stuff and all drinking after that flows from it being forced upon him by the demands of society. Of course, it does not help that his stepfather is a drinker and a gambler and takes young Jack to the saloons with him. At seven years old, Jack gets into a situation where he is given drinks by some Italians. His mother has placed in him a fear of the local Italian immigrants and so he drinks until he can barely stand. Once at home, he is in bed for days in a delirium. In this delirium, he "wandered deep beneath the ground through a thousand of these dens [of iniquity], and . . . when I would come upon my father, seated at table in these subterranean crypts, gambling with Chinese for great stakes of gold, all my outrage gave vent in the vilest cursing."[4] This delirium proves his close association with saloons even from that early age.

As Jack grows older and begins to hang out on the waterfront, he, too, becomes a regular at the saloons. At first, he drinks only when someone buys him drinks. One day, he realizes that not only is he expected to accept the drinks of his drinking buddies (which he has done freely for some time), he is supposed to buy a round for everyone. He takes this lesson to heart, buying drinks along with everyone else. When he has money, he spends it freely in the bars. London claims that he was called the "Prince of the Oyster Pirates" because of his open hand with his money in the waterfront saloons. As a result of these early experiences, London concludes that to drink is synonymous with manliness, making it a somewhat wholesome form of camaraderie. He reasons, "In the saloons life was different. Men talked with great voices, laughed great laughs, and there was an atmosphere of greatness. Here was something more than common every-day where nothing happened."[5] Even as London moves away from the waterfront and enters into more polite society, he sees the same thing: sharing a drink with another is a way to break down barriers and make fast friends. He uses this bit of social etiquette over and over again throughout his life to swap stories or get information.

At one point, London promises Charmian he will stop drinking altogether. After an appalling binge in New York followed by a sober trip around Cape Horn, London decides that social drinking is, in fact, okay, and that he will continue to drink socially, but that alcohol will not master him. He concludes, "No, I decided; I shall take my drink on occasion . . . I decided coolly and deliberately that I should continue to do what I had been trained to do! I would drink—but, oh, more skillfully, more discreetly, than ever before."[6]

His lowest point comes during a period he calls the Long Sickness. He feels depressed and defeated. He begins having conversations with what he terms the White Logic of his brain. The White Logic holds that life is futile, yet it will not release man to death. It longs to live, even if existence means pain or misery. London, always on the adventure trail, argues for life. It takes months before he comes out of the Long Sickness. He says that the two things that saved him are socialism and the love of a woman, Charmian. By the end of the book, he finally admits that John Barleycorn has indeed mastered him. All those years of claiming freedom to stop whenever he wanted have led to bondage. He became a heavy drinker and never stopped, even toward the end when he knew that it would shorten his life.

Promoting Temperance

In the first chapter, London's stated reason for writing the book is that he hopes it will become a Prohibitionist tract. He believes that "[w]hen the women get the ballot, they will vote for prohibition. . . It is the wives, and sisters, and mothers, and they only, who will drive the nails into the coffin of John Barleycorn."[7] The Prohibition Party, the Christian Temperance Union, and the Women's Temperance Christian Union all promoted the book within their organizations.

This book is another good example of the way London knew his audience and catered to them. Even though the book is all about his drinking lifestyle, in the end he will not change it. He suggests that this book will help those future generations not yet born—both the men and the women who suffer with the men—to avoid the pain that John Barleycorn inflicts. He is unrepentant of his own sins, but he puts forth the hope that his confession will help others with theirs.

Losing the Battle

London's personification of alcohol as a reasoning being lends an interesting flavor to the book. The struggle seems to be against a force fighting back rather than an inert substance. The amazing thing is the transparency with which London shows his struggles.

Looking back now, almost a hundred years later, London's fight with John Barleycorn shows the typical patterns of an alcoholic's life. Even Charmian, in her diaries, shows the typical response of an alcoholic's partner.[8] London was not the kind of alcoholic who drank himself into oblivion. Instead, he was the social drinker who could not stop. His social life was tied to drink, or at least he perceived it that way. He claimed, "The desire for alcohol is quite peculiarly mental in its origin. It is a matter of mental training and growth, and it is cultivated in social soil."[9] Toward the end of the book he reminisces about how he traveled the world, drink in hand—and that given the chance, he would not change that.

London's insistence in the first three-quarters of the book that he drinks solely for social reasons and that he really doesn't like the taste of it makes his eventual admission that John Barleycorn has defeated him even more potent. "And right there John Barleycorn had me. I was beginning to drink regularly. I was beginning to drink alone."[10] Where once he thought he had control, he lost.

Although modern scholars appreciate London's full body of work, early biographers claimed London's later works were far inferior to his early work. Some attribute it to his increased drinking, others to his demands on himself to simply produce writing to fund his various activities and responsibilities. Either way, he did not reduce his drinking as he grew older. Rather, he increased it. His final realization that he had a problem came at the ranch.

Environmental Pieces

In a final twist of the kaleidoscope, London and Charmian returned to Beauty Ranch in California after their recovery in Australia. London's third life change, a return to the land, was about to blossom. After experiencing the ravaging diseases and white imperialism of the South Seas, he decided that the closest he would ever get to heaven on earth would be in Sonoma Valley. He found his Eden in his own backyard.[1] He became a dedicated farmer, seeking ways to increase the yield of the land. He stated, "By using my head, my judgment, and all the latest knowledge in the matter of farming, I have pledged myself, my manhood, my fortune, my books and all I possess to this undertaking."[2]

London's primary goal was to apply science to farming for increased yield of crops and best breeding. On his ranch he pioneered in soil conservation, using tillage and terracing to make the worn-out hillside lands fruitful again. He raised vegetables, grains, alfalfa, grapes, fruit trees, prunes, potatoes, spineless cactus, eucalyptus trees, horses, goats, chickens, hogs, beef, dairy cattle, and prize-winning livestock. And he cut the biggest and best hay crops in Sonoma County.[3] Within the first year of his return, in 1910, London began construction on his dream home, Wolf House. As always, his current life experiences found their way into his stories.

Nature Versus Man: "All Gold Canyon"

Several of London's stories from this point on revolve around events in and around Sonoma Valley, with an emphasis on nature as the benevolent source of life. The emphasis switches from man against nature (where nature is the protagonist) to man against nature (where nature is the victim of man's senseless abuse).[4] The earliest example of this theme appears in the short story "All Gold Canyon" (1906), written just after London purchased his first tract of land for Beauty Ranch. The setting is a canyon in the virgin wilderness of California. A miner comes into the canyon, desecrating it in his search for gold. He finds his gold but almost dies when a dark stranger tries to steal it. He kills the stranger instead. Once the miner

London and his horse at Beauty Ranch

has what he wants, he continues on, leaving his marks on the canyon. London dramatizes his exit using phrases such as "a ripping and tearing of vines and boughs" and "a clashing of steel-shod hoofs on stone."[5] Once the miner is gone, London uses words like "crept," "drowsed," "whispered," and "fluttered" to describe the canyon returning back to its peaceful state.

This theme of nature as victim demonstrates a profound shift in London's thinking about nature. Looking at his adventures and the writing that resulted, "his career might well be studied as a lifelong series of attempts to escape the corruptions of civilization and to recapture the simple, maternal security of nature."[6] His escape to the wilderness and jungle brought only hardship. His Sonoma Valley stories show that he was close to finding his ideal of nature.

Return to the Soil: *Burning Daylight*

This change in attitude toward the environment shows up in three of his novels written after his return from the South Seas. The first, *Burning Daylight* (1910), starts in the Yukon, moves to the city, and then to Sonoma Valley. Burning Daylight is the main character, a man shaped by the rugged environment of the Yukon. He leaves the Northland for San Francisco, where he becomes a successful businessman. He falls in love with his secretary, Dede Mason, and proposes. She refuses him until he finds a new lease on life through escape to the country, emphasizing London's theme of return to the soil for healing restoration.

True to form, London incorporates much of his own experience into this story. Burning Daylight and Dede live on a ranch much like Beauty Ranch, and Dede is much like Charmian. Dede is the driving force behind the success of the ranch. One biographer writes, "The book was . . . a remarkable reaffirmation of Jack's love for Charmian and his optimism about their life in the country."[7]

Critics at the time panned *Burning Daylight*. It seems they never wanted London to leave the Northland. When it was released in 1910, the *New York Times* reported, "The moment [London] steps out of the region where the human animal is pitted against the primal forces of nature in the wilderness, at that moment he loses all grip of the creature and writes of him or her rather more crudely—as to comprehension—than the average schoolboy would."[8] The public was not so disappointed. They liked the love story with a happy ending, buying enough copies of the book to equal one quarter of the total sold for *The Sea-Wolf*.[9]

A Series of Tragedies

The same year *Burning Daylight* was published, Charmian gave birth to a baby girl. The baby died within hours. Charmian got pregnant again in 1912 but miscarried. She was informed that she would never be able to have children. This ended all hope for an heir for Jack London. He had hoped to pass on his newly acquired property and farming techniques to his sons. This hope highlights yet another departure from socialist thinking.

In 1913 another misfortune occurred. London's dream home, Wolf House, burned down only days before it was ready for occupancy. At the time, the fire was blamed on arson. Many years later it was determined that the fire was actually caused by the combustion of some rags left in the home. The house was not insured and London never tried to rebuild it. He and Charmian continued to live in the same cottage they had occupied since settling on the ranch, until his death.

Rejection of Socialism: *The Valley of the Moon*

London wrote two more books featuring locations similar to Beauty Ranch. The first, *The Valley of the Moon* (1913), tells the story of a laundry girl who marries a professional boxer turned teamster. They long to escape from city life and eventually find their Eden in the Valley of the Moon.[10] The story is told in three parts. Book I details the courtship of Saxon and Billy Roberts. London explores their working-class status, emphasizing their hard labor and the callous treatment they receive. Saxon works in a laundry facility, ironing fancy starched clothes for the middle class. Billy works as a teamster, driving horses for a local stable. Book I describes their marriage against the backdrop of union strikes in Oakland, California, where they live. Initially, Billy Roberts exhibits faith in socialism, trusting that the workers' rebellion will break the will of the capitalists. When Billy gets thrown in jail for beating up strike breakers and Saxon has a miscarriage after witnessing violence in the streets, Saxon decides it is time to leave Oakland. Billy agrees to go, his faith in socialism as an agent of change now dead.

Biographers see the first two parts of this book as London's justification for accepting then rejecting the socialist cause. From London's earliest interest in socialism, there were glimpses of disparity between the ideals of socialism and London's writing and lifestyle. In spite of his rugged spirit of individualism, he still believed that socialism was the answer to the evils of capitalism. At first, London believed in a passive approach to building the socialist movement. Later, especially after his time in London's East End, he became more of a revolutionary. He eventually resigned from the Socialist Party, citing their loss of interest in revolution.

Book III documents the travels of Billy and Saxon as they roam the California countryside in search of land for farming. They talk a lot about how their forebears crossed the plains to arrive in California. As they wander, they come across immigrants who have moved to California in more recent years, acquiring land and farming it better than the original immigrants who came across the prairies. Saxon asks lots of questions, studying their methods for producing higher crop yields. They eventually come to Sonoma Valley and find their perfect piece of land. The story ends with Saxon announcing she is pregnant, emphasizing the potential of their new start in life.

The main theme of the novel, escape from the working class into the pastoral dream, closely follows London's own path and desires. Like London, Billy and Saxon Roberts buy land in the Valley of the Moon and farm it using the latest scientific research. Like many of London's heroines, Saxon Roberts is based on Charmian. Saxon embodies the New Woman. It is she who makes the decision to move away from the city and she who advocates scientific farming.

There are a few problems with the novel. The storyline is predictable and the story becomes overburdened with information that does not move the story along. This probably comes from London trying to recount too much of his own life in the novel: his time at Carmel, his positive and negative responses to the immigrants, the details of scientific farming, and so on. In spite of these problems, London manages to work several themes into the novel. One, discussed earlier, is London's justification for becoming a capitalist. The second theme centers on a return to the land, complete with lessons on scientific farming and land conservation. The most poignant theme—and the one most likely to grip his readers—is that of losing faith and finding a new dream.

An Unsatisfactory Ending: *The Little Lady of the Big House*

The last Sonoma Valley book, *The Little Lady of the Big House* (1916), features a love triangle that plays itself out on the large, successful ranch of Dick and Paula Forrest. Dick has poured himself into the running of the ranch, leaving little time for his wife. Paula takes refuge in the arms of Evan Graham, an artistic and sensitive man. When Dick finds out, he makes Paula choose between them. Paula, in love with both of them, chooses suicide to solve the problem.

London often thought his latest book would be completely different than anything else he had written or that was already on the market. This book was no exception. Once again, the critics attacked his work. The *Dial* wrote, "For interesting it certainly is not, after the first few pages."[11] The *Nation* wrote, "He does not achieve reality or sincerity in this performance."[12] Even modern critics have a hard time finding the good in this novel. The sexual overtones are too stark and the unhappy ending leaves the love triangle unresolved. After this book, London turned away from his agricultural themes. His never-ending pursuit of knowledge led him in new directions.

The Kaleidoscope Is Complete

In his last year, 1916, London was plagued by problems but remained excited and energized by new directions in his writing and new philosophies on the horizon. His last stories indicate he was on his way to yet another life change. He was starting to incorporate the ideas of Swiss psychiatrist Carl Jung into his writing, evident in his last story, "The Water Baby."

During his last few months, London suffered from severe rheumatism and uremia. His kidneys were failing, and nothing short of a radical lifestyle change would help. He spent the first seven months of the year in Hawaii to rest and recover his health. Against his doctors' orders, he never stopped his heavy drinking.

Things at the ranch were going badly, too. His prize stallion died, and he went to trial over water rights on his land. Toward the end, he complained of insomnia. When the inevitable occurred, the doctors' report read:

> At 6:30 PM, November 21, 1916, Jack London partook of his dinner. He was taken during the night with what was supposed to be an acute attack of indigestion. This, however, proved to be gastrointestinal uraemia. He lapsed into coma and died at 7:45 PM, November 22.
>
> Dr. W.S. Porter
> Dr. A.M. Thompson
> Dr. W.B. Hays
> Dr. J.W. Shiels[13]

Perhaps London would appreciate the irony of his life, that "after striving so long and so hard to break out from the underworld of the work beast, he succeeded in working himself to death."[14] But he died as he wished—still going strong in pursuing his passions in life.

A Few More Pieces

Because of his work habits and his prolific pen, London had five books ready to publish when he died. They were all published by Macmillan in the next couple of years. Three of these, *The Human Drift*, *Jerry of the Islands*, and *Michael Brother of Jerry* have received little attention from scholars. The other two include stories considered to have the depth of his earliest works. *On the Makaloa Mat,* a collection of Hawaiian short stories, includes "The Water Baby," the last story London ever wrote. In it he uses many symbols from Carl Jung's philosophies, showing that he was finally leaving the realm of realism and embracing spirituality.[15] London may have been on the edge of yet another major life change with his renewed interest in spirituality.

His novella *The Red One* (1918), from the book of the same name, demonstrates that his creative genius was still in full force at the end of his life, as was his continual search for answers and changing philosophy. In this science fiction-like story, a red orb lands in the jungle and becomes a god to the natives. The natives, over generations, offer human sacrifices to this orb. When struck with a pole, it emits a haunting sound. A scientist visiting the island desires to see what it is that makes this sound. No islander will help him, for they risk death if they reveal its location.

Eventually the scientist catches a fever, but the medicine man of the village will not help him. The medicine man's only desire is to see the scientist die so he can have his head for his devil-devil hut. Dying of the fever, the scientist manages to finagle a way to see what makes the sound. As his dying moment draws near, he feels he has discovered a great mystery that he must share with the world. But this is not to be. Instead, his last vision is of his head twirling slowly in the hut of the medicine man.

The storyline of *The Red One* follows the classic hero outline but falls a couple of steps short of the final stages of the journey. Because the story ends at the moment of enlightenment without going on to resurrection and return, it leaves the piece open to interpretation. Scholars have interpreted it both negatively (where the scientist is disillusioned, focusing on the twirling head), and positively (where the scientist is finally enlightened). It is fitting that at the time London was in the middle of his own search for truth and was, in fact, dying. London had recently read Jung and was exploring the idea of the collective unconscious, represented in this story by the red orb. London died without being able to share what he felt were the revelations of Jung's theories, just as the hero in *The Red One* died before sharing his.

In 1922 Macmillan published *Dutch Courage and Other Stories*. This book is a collection of London's very early stories, with an introduction by Charmian. Still later, in 1963, an unfinished novel, *The Assassination Bureau*, was completed by Robert L. Fish and published by McGraw.

A Life Well Lived

London's willingness to bare his soul to his readers, or at least the soul he thought they wanted to read about, endeared him to the public. His life of adventure attracted free spirits and adventurers across the nation. And his willingness to stand up for the underdog endeared him to the common man around the world. In his day, London was popular and was regularly in the news for both his writing and his adventures. But as an author, the full body of his work was not fully appreciated until the latter half of the twentieth century. With the perspective of time, there has been a greater appreciation of London's literary talent and his contributions to an understanding of the cultural environment of turn-of-the-century California.

LONDON'S LEGACY

J ack London once stated, "The proper function of man is to
  live, not to exist. I shall not waste my days in trying to prolong them. I shall use my time."[1] Because he practiced what he
preached, London accomplished many things and his legacy
is manifold. His influence today ranges far beyond his literary
accomplishments.

Many of the pieces of London's life were documented
through his writing, articles about him, or in papers that
Charmian saved. With each twist of his kaleidoscope, a
different impact of his work is reflected back to the viewer.
For example, London contributed to American literature and
functioned as a cultural hero. He photographed a changing
and war-torn world, leaving an archive of important historical
photos. His ranch has become a state park, preserving some
of his agricultural work. The city of Oakland honored him
by naming a retail section after him. A quick search of the
web shows that many people still read London's work and are
inspired by his life. References to his novel *The Iron Heel* were
recognized throughout the Occupy Wall Street Movement of
2011.

London embodied the great American Hero through his
bold adventures, first in the Klondike and then across the
globe. His adventurous lifestyle, his political position as a
socialist, and his prolific writing put him squarely in the
public's view. Readers couldn't seem to get enough of his

London in 1916

stories and the stories about his life. He is often considered to be the first American celebrity. That sense of celebrity lives on today through a vast collection of material related to his life.

The Huntington Collection

Because London's life and pursuits were well-documented, he left behind a rich resource for future generations. When London married Charmian in 1905, she began to collect the memorabilia of their life together. Her collection included drafts of Jack's writing, photos, correspondence with their many friends, letters to publishers, royalty statements and her personal diaries, as well as souvenirs and items purchased on their travels.

After London died, Charmian began looking for a place to house some of their collection. The Huntington Library in San Marino, California, purchased some of Jack's papers in early 1920. Over the next sixty years, they continued to make purchases from Beauty Ranch and their collection grew to around sixty thousand items, including ten thousand photographs of the Londons' travels and the ranch. It is the largest Jack London collection in the world. The collection is made available to researchers who publish scholarly material on London.

Other Collections

There are a few other notable collections that are more narrowly focused, offering even more insight into London's work. Sonoma State University has a collection that focuses on the first appearances of his work in magazines and posters from movies made from London's books. These items came from the private collections of two local individuals who had an interest in London.

Utah State University houses the second largest collection of London's manuscripts. The university began its collection in the 1960s as the outgrowth of the relationship between a professor at the school and London's nephew and executor of his estate. The initial purchase contained the first-edition novels that London inscribed to his wife, Charmian. Other notable items are a logbook from the *Snark*, his Russo-Japanese correspondent's notebook, and the plots London purchased from Sinclair Lewis. This collection is open to all researchers.

There are two other noteworthy places to conduct London research. One is Centenary College of Louisiana. This college is home to the Jack London Museum and Research Center. Earle Labor, Centenary's emeritus professor of American literature, is the director. Labor is the pre-eminent London scholar, known worldwide for his research. He has written ten books on London and dozens of articles. The other place is The Bancroft Library at the University of California, Berkeley. The Bancroft has an extensive collection of London material available online.

London's Photography

London's travels led him to historically important places. He documented his trips in words and in photography. He took or acquired pictures in the Klondike during the brief gold rush there. When the Great Earthquake of 1906 hit San Francisco, he and Charmian rode into the area and photographed what they saw. Both of the Londons were able photographers. In Hawaii, their photos captured the time of transition from a strictly Polynesian culture to a more American one. His photos from the Solomon Islands are notable for their natural settings. Professional photos from that time were typically

EYEWITNESS REPORT, FIRE, SAN FRANCISCO, 1906

Jack London was a journalist and photographer as well as an author. When the earthquake of 1906 hit San Francisco, Jack and Charmian London rode into the city on horseback. As he looked at the devastation, London commented to Charmian that he would never write about what he saw because words would be insufficient. However, when *Collier's* asked him to cover it for a substantial amount of money, he managed to write a 2,500-word article. His most poignant descriptions are of the poor and working class leaving the city in a section of the article called "A Caravan of Trunks":

> All night these tens of thousands fled before the flames. Many of them, the poor people from the labor ghetto, had fled all day as well. They had left their homes burdened with possessions. Now and again they lightened up, flinging out upon the street clothing and treasures they had dragged for miles.
>
> They held on longest to their trunks, and over these trunks many a strong man broke his heart that night. The hills of San Francisco are steep, and up these hills, mile after mile, were the trunks dragged. Everywhere were trunks with across them lying their exhausted owners, men and women. Before the march of the flames were flung picket lines of soldiers. And a block at a time, as the flames advanced, these pickets retreated. One of their tasks was to keep the trunk-pullers moving. The exhausted creatures, stirred on by the menace of bayonets, would arise and struggle up the steep pavements, pausing from weakness every five or ten feet.
>
> Often, after surmounting a heart-breaking hill. they would find another wall of flame advancing upon them at right angles and be compelled to change anew the line of their retreat. In the end, completely played out, after toiling for a dozen hours like giants, thousands of them were compelled to abandon their trunks. Here the shopkeepers and soft members of the middle class were at a disadvantage. But the working-men dug holes in vacant lots and backyards and buried their trunks.[2]

posed in studios, so London's work is valuable for its candid capturing of everyday life. He photographed scenes from two wars, the Russo-Japanese War and the Mexican-American War.

Sonoma Valley

Sonoma Valley is home to London's Beauty Ranch. In 1963, some of the land was donated for a state park. The park includes the ruins of London's dream home, Wolf House, burned in a fire, and a nineteenth-century winery, damaged in the Great San Francisco Earthquake of 1906. You can also visit his silos, barns, and the famous Pig Palace that London designed to allow a two-hundred-pig feeding operation run by

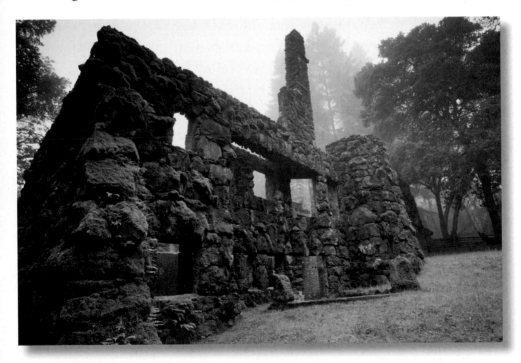

The remains of London's beloved Wolf House, which burned down in 1913, can be seen at Jack London Historical Park in Northern California.

one person. For literary fans, the highlight of the ranch may be the cottage where Jack and Charmian lived during their time on the ranch. Visitors can also see the contoured terraces and the lake he created on the property. Docents at The Cottage and adjacent Stone Dining Room help you relive the days of London and Charmian and dive into their lifestyle. Over the years, the park has also held workshops for teachers.

London had several successes on Beauty Ranch. He installed the first hollow-block silo in the West. He used terracing to conserve water and reduce erosion. He designed a system of removing waste from his barns and pig palace, collecting the manure to use as fertilizer, a practice he learned by reading about how Chinese farmers maintained productive land for generations. In California, the first homesteaders simply used the soil without replenishing it until the farm was bankrupt. London purchased several of these worn-out farms and turned them back to productivity. He was one of the first soil conservationists.

Next to the park is the Kenwood Winery, run by the same family that operated Beauty Ranch for the Londons from the time of Jack London through Charmian's death. The winery was established in 1976. They use grapes from London's terraced vineyards in addition to other grapes grown in Sonoma Valley to produce the Jack London series of wine. Because London used his ranch as an experimental farm, his vineyards were planned for family consumption rather than for profit.

Oakland

London spent much of his childhood in Oakland, California, and the surrounding bay area. One year after his death, the city dedicated an oak tree to his memory. It can still be seen in the Frank Ogawa Plaza and is nicknamed "The Jack London Oak." Another London landmark is Jack London Square, a combination of retail, business, and entertainment establishments. A tiny log cabin sits in the square, reconstructed from the actual logs of the cabin where London stayed during the White Silence. Visitors can peek inside the windows and get an idea of how people had to live during such times. A life-sized bronze statue of Jack London greets visitors to the waterfront.

One other highlight of the area is Heinhold's First and Last Chance Saloon, later nicknamed Jack London's Rendezvous. London would come to the bar as a schoolboy to study. The owner of the bar admired London and lent him the money to pay for his college tuition. Heinhold said this about London, "He just jumped into life with both feet in that courageous way of his, and he got romance and mystery and beauty out of it where other men could see only labor. That's genius."[3] London gathered considerable material for his writing by listening to the sailors that frequented the saloon. The building still contains much of its original interior and other artifacts. London fans come to sit at "Jack's table" and try to soak up some of his genius. A Jack London mural on the outside pays tribute to this famous son of Oakland.

International Audience

From the beginning, London had an international following. That enthusiasm continues today. A group of self-defined German "aficionados and experts" maintain a website[4] in cooperation with Jack London's heirs and descendants (www. jacklondon.org). The website highlights materials not easily located elsewhere on the web, such as the eulogy written by a friend he met in the Klondike whose dog was the model for Buck in *The Call of the Wild*. There are links to Jack London

A statue of London stands in Jack London Square in Oakland, California.

information and websites from other countries, not just the United States. Many of the essays on the site are written from the perspective of other cultures. Despite these other interpretations of London's work, it still remains relevant. As testament to his popularity, his work has been translated into seventy languages.

Cultural Relevance Today

Jack London references and reflections can be found all over the web. In addition to scholarly works, there are many references to and analyses of London. For example, London seems to have found a special place in the heart of the blog writers for Art of Manliness, the largest independent men's interest magazine on the web. Readers can enjoy entries such as a "manvotional" of London's "On the Writer's Philosophy of Life;" a description of manhood, which is really a description of Jack London in the Klondike; and a ten-part series that is a case study of London's *thumos*,[5] a reference to the noble part of Plato's tripartite soul.

London's views as a socialist, as presented in his novel *The Iron Heel*, are found through articles and interviews related to the political movement in America called Occupy Wall Street. The picture of an oppressive oligarchy (power by a few), in the form of government and corporate collaboration, as an iron heel smashing the average

> **tripartite soul**
>
> Plato's division of the psyche into three parts: The appetitive mind, or physical desires, identified as the black horse on the left; the spirited (*thumos*) mind that seeks for high moral ground, identified as the white horse on the right; and the rational mind, the charioteer that (hopefully) keeps the chariot and horses under control.

worker resounds with those trying to bring attention to what they feel is an out-of-control power structure.

For the serious London enthusiast or scholar, several groups maintain ongoing publications. An international reference website has already been mentioned. In America, the Jack London Society maintains a thorough connection to all events and publications Jack London-related.

For a more casual acquaintance with London, try the Jack London Author page on Facebook maintained by Random House publishers.[6] They post regularly, sharing historical information, current events, and original photographs from London's travels. For an interactive experience, try the iClassics Collection app titled iLondon: The Immersive Jack London Experience.[7] The app includes several unedited London texts. Illustrations and music have been added, as well as interactive features. It was released in 2016 to coincide with the one-hundredth anniversary of London's death.

Continued Scholarship

London scholars continue to pour forth lectures, articles, and books on Jack London's life and works. For example, in 2013, London scholar Clarice Stasz published a book titled *Jack London's Women*, a look at the tight circle of influential women in the writer's life. London's fascinating life, plus the seemingly never-ending kaleidoscope of material available, guarantees that this will continue far into the future. His personal philosophies and lifestyle still inspire students and hobbyists alike. As short story writer Katherine Mansfield, one of his contemporaries, noted, "He is one of those writers who win the affection of their readers—who are, in themselves, the favourite book."[8]

CHRONOLOGY

1876– John Griffith Chaney is born in San Francisco on January 12. His mother, Flora, marries John London on September 7.

1891– Graduates from grammar school. Holds various jobs, including factory worker (cannery), oyster pirate, and California Fish Patrol.

1893– Works aboard the *Sophia Sutherland* as an able-bodied seaman during sealing voyage. Wins first prize in newspaper contest for "Story of a Typhoon Off the Coast of Japan."

1895– Returns to high school at age nineteen.

1896– Joins Socialist Labor Party. Attends the University of California, Berkeley, for one semester before dropping out.

1897– Begins speaking for socialist causes. Joins the gold rush to the Klondike. John London dies.

1898– Returns from the Klondike with scurvy. Begins writing career in earnest.

1899– Begins publishing short stories in the *Overland Monthly*.

1900– Marries Bessie Maddern on April 7. First book published, *The Son of the Wolf*, a collection of short stories that appeared in *Overland Monthly*.

1901– First daughter, Joan, is born.

1902– Spends eight weeks in London's East End researching material for *The People of The Abyss*. Second daughter, Becky, is born.

1903– *The Call of the Wild* is published, catapulting London to worldwide fame. Separates from Bessie Maddern.

1904– Travels to Japan and Korea to report on the Russo-Japanese War for Hearst Syndicate. *The Sea-Wolf* is published.

1905 — Buys first tract of land for Beauty Ranch near Glen Ellen in Sonoma Valley. Marries Charmian Kittredge.

1906 — Begins building the *Snark*. Publishes *White Fang*.

1907 — Sails from San Francisco in the *Snark* with wife, Charmian, and crew.

1908 — *The Iron Heel* is published.

1909 — Abandons *Snark* trip. *Martin Eden* is published.

1910 — Begins building Wolf House, his dream home. Daughter Joy is born; she dies thirty-eight hours after birth. Publishes *Burning Daylight*.

1912 — Charmian has a miscarriage, ending the couples' hopes of having children. Publishes *The House of Pride*.

1913 — Wolf House burns down. Publishes *John Barleycorn* and *The Valley of the Moon*.

1914 — Reports for *Collier's* on the Mexican Revolution.

1915 — Goes to Hawaii to recover health. *The Star Rover* is published.

1916 — Resigns from Socialist Party. Publishes *The Little Lady of the Big House*.

1916 — Dies from gastrointestinal uremia on November 22.

1931 — *The Call of the Wild* is awarded the Newberry Medal.

1986 — London is honored by the United States Postal Service with a twenty-five-cent postage stamp in the Great Americans series.

2000 — Named one of the "Top 100 Writers of the 20th Century" by *Writers Digest* magazine.

2014 — Earle Labor's biography *Jack London: An American Life* wins the Andrew Carnegie Medal for Excellence in nonfiction.

CHAPTER NOTES

Chapter 1. Looking Through a Kaleidoscope

1. Alfred Kazin, as quoted in Earle Labor and Jeanne Campbell Reesman, *Twayne's United States Authors Series: Jack London, Revised Edition* (New York: Twayne Publishers, 1994), p. 1.
2. John Perry, *Jack London: An American Myth* (Chicago: Nelson-Hall, 1981), p. 111.
3. Irving Stone, *Jack London: Sailor on Horseback* (New York: Doubleday and Company, 1956), p. 68.
4. Edgar Allen Poe defined a short story as one that could be read in one sitting in his essay "The Philosophy of Composition" in 1846.
5. The Huntington Library, Art Collections, and Botanical Gardens, http://www.huntington.org. Photocopies of much of London's personal correspondence and his notes can be found on this website.
6. Perry, p. 85.
7. *Twayne's*, p. 38.
8. "Social Darwinism," Definitions, 2016, http://www.definitions.net/definition/social%20darwinism (accessed November 23, 2016).
9. Jack London, "In A Far County," *The Portable Jack London*, Earle Labor, ed. (New York: Penguin Books, 1994), p. 11.
10. Robert Peluso, "Gazing at Royalty" in *Rereading Jack London*, Leonard Cassuto and Jeanne Campbell Reesman, eds. (Stanford: Stanford University Press, 1996), p. 58.
11. Perry, p. 148.
12. Jack London, *The Sea-Wolf* (New York: Macmillan, 1931), p. 155.
13. *Twayne's*, p. 38.

Chapter 2. Pieces of Personal History

1. Irving Stone, *Jack London: Sailor on Horseback* (New York: Doubleday and Company, 1978), p. 31.
2. Jack London, *The Sea-Wolf* (New York: Macmillan, 1931), p. 155.

3. London's review of *The Jungle* in *Wilshire's Magazine* in 1906 is most easily obtained in *Jack London: American Rebel*, ed. Philip S. Foner (New York: Citadel, 1947): 517–524.

4. Brian J. Cantwell, "Why Russians flock to Jack London's California ranch 100 years after his death, " *Seattle Times*, June 12, 2016, http://www.seattletimes.com/life/travel/why-russians-flock-to-jack-londons-california-ranch-100-years-after-his-death/.

5. Jack London, "What Life Means to Me," *The Portable Jack London*, Earle Labor, ed. (New York: Penguin Books, 1994), p. 478.

6. Cecilia Tichi, *Jack London: A Writer's Fight for a Better America*. (Chapel Hill, NC: The University of North Carolina Press, 2015), p. 47.

7. Clarice Stasz, *Jack London's Women* (Amherst, MA: University of Massachusetts Press, 2013), p. 30.

8. Alex Kershaw, *Jack London: A Life* (New York: St. Martin's Press, 1997), p. 66.

9. Franklin Walker, *Jack London & the Klondike* (California: The Huntington Library, 1966), pp. 88–90.

Chapter 3. Pieces of the Northland

1. Daniel Dyer, *Jack London: A Biography* (New York: Scholastic, Inc., 1997), p. 107.

2. "Wolf" is the name given to the white man by the Indians of Alaska.

3. Earle Labor, *Jack London: An American Life* (New York: Farrar, Straus and Giroux, 2013), p. 139

4. Jack London, "The White Silence" in *Jack London: Novels and Stories* (New York: The Library of America, 1958), p. 301.

5. Earle Labor and Jeanne Campbell Reesman, *Twayne's United States Authors Series: Jack London*, rev. ed. (New York: Twayne Publishers, 1994), p. 26.

6. Jack London. "To Build a Fire" in *Short Stories of Jack London*, Earle Labor, ed. (New York: Macmillan Publishing Company, 1990), p. 283.
7. Ibid., p. 289.
8. Ibid., p. 290.
9. Ibid., p. 295.
10. James Lundquist, *Jack London: Adventures, Ideas, and Fiction* (New York: Continuum, 1990), p. 95.

Chapter 4. First Major Success

1. Clarice Stasz, *American Dreamers: Charmian and Jack London* (New York: St. Martin's Press, 1988), p. 110.
2. Earle Labor, *Jack London: An American Life* (New York: Farrar, Straus and Giroux, 2013), p. 158
3. Jack London, *The Call of the Wild* (New York: Macmillan Publishing Company), 1994, p. 12.
4. Ibid., p. 16.
5. Ibid., p. 46.
6. Ibid., p. 62.
7. Ibid., p. 84.
8. Ibid., p. 85.
9. Ibid.
10. Ibid., p. 108.
11. Ibid., p. 116.
12. Ibid., p. 118.
13. James Lundquist, *Jack London: Adventures, Ideas, and Fiction* (New York: Continuum, 1990), p. 107.
14. These stages are based on Joseph Campbell's book *The Hero With a Thousand Faces*.

Chapter 5. Pieces of the World

1. Jack London, *The Iron Heel*. Footnote in Chapter xvi.
2. Jack London, *The Abyss*, chapter 24.
3. Earle Labor, *Jack London: An American Life* (New York: Farrar, Straus and Giroux, 2013), p. 164.

4. Ibid.

5. Jonathan Auerbach, "Congested Mails" in *Rereading Jack London*, Leonard Cassuto and Jeanne Campbell Reesman, eds. (Stanford: Stanford University Press, 1996), p. 37.

6. Alex Kershaw, *Jack London: A Life* (New York: St. Martin's Press, 1997), p. 120.

7. John Perry, *Jack London: An American Myth* (Chicago: Nelson-Hall, 1981), p. 281.

8. Kershaw, p. 143.

Chapter 6. A Story of Redemption

1. Clarice Stasz, *Jack London's Women* (Amherst, MA: University of Massachusetts Press, 2013), p. 30.

2. Jack London, *The Sea-Wolf and Other Stories* (New York: Penguin Books, 1989), p. 34.

3. "Getting Into Print" *Editor*, March 1903.

4. Letter to Max E. Feckler, October 26, 1914

5. "Getting Into Print."

6. Jack London, *The Sea-Wolf and Other Stories*, p. 274.

7. John Perry, *Jack London: An American Myth* (Chicago: Nelson-Hall, 1981), p. 79.

8. Sam S. Baskett, "Sea Change in 'The Sea-Wolf'" in *Rereading Jack London*, Leonard Cassuto and Jeanne Campbell Reesman, eds. (Stanford: Stanford University Press, 1996), p. 108.

9. Earle Labor and Jeanne Campbell Reesman, *Twayne's United States Authors Series: Jack London*, Revised Edition (New York: Twayne Publishers, 1994), p. 60.

Chapter 7. Appeasing His Readers

1. Alex Kershaw, *Jack London: A Life* (New York: St. Martin's Press, 1997), p. 155.

2. Jack London, *White Fang* (New York: Viking, 1999), p. 84.

3. Ibid., p. 109.

4. Ibid., p. 149.

Chapter 8. Pieces of Adventures on the High Seas

1. Jack London, *The Cruise of the Snark* (New York: Sheridan House, 1971, 4th impression 1996), p. 3.

2. London, *The Cruise of the Snark*, pp. 339–340.

3. Jack London, *The House of Pride*, "Koolau the Leper," http://london.sonoma.edu/Writings/HousePride/koolau.html (accessed February 9, 2017).

4. Jack London, "Koolau the Leper" in *The Portable Jack London*, Earle Labor, ed. (New York: Penguin Books, 1994), p. 164.

5. Ibid.

6. James Slagel, "Political Leprosy" in *Rereading Jack London*, Leonard Cassuto and Jeanne Campbell Reesman, eds. (Stanford: Stanford University Press, 1996), p. 185.

7. Jack London, *South Seas Tales* (New York: Dover Publications, 2001), pp. 47–48.

8. Earle Labor and Jeanne Campbell Reesman, *Twayne's United States Authors Series: Jack London*, rev. ed. (New York: Twayne Publishers, 1994), p. 92.

Chapter 9. Biographical Bits

1. Jack London, *John Barleycorn or, Alcoholic Memoirs* (New York: Penguin Group, 1990), p. 126.

2. Jack London, *Martin Eden* (New York: Penguin Books, 1993), p. 482.

3. John Perry, *Jack London: An American Myth* (Chicago: Nelson-Hall, 1981), p. 296.

4. London, *John Barleycorn*, p. 32.

5. Ibid., p. 38.

6. Ibid., pp. 236–237.

7. Ibid., p. 15.

8. Clarice Stasz, *American Dreamers: Charmian and Jack London* (New York: St. Martin's Press, 1988), pp. 231–232.

9. London, *John Barleycorn*, pp. 234–235.

10. Ibid., pp. 190–191.

Chapter 10. Environmental Pieces

1. Earle Labor and Jeanne Campbell Reesman, *Twayne's United States Authors Series: Jack London, Revised Edition* (New York: Twayne Publishers, 1994), p. 92.

2. Cecilia Tichi, *Jack London: A Writer's Fight for a Better America.* (Chapel Hill, NC: The University of North Carolina Press, 2015), p. 158.

3. Jack London's Beauty Ranch, "Jack London the Visionary." https://web.archive.org/web/20160503021115/http://www. jacklondons.net/intro.html (accessed January 31, 2017).

4. *Twayne's*, p. 96.

5. Jack London, "All Gold Canyon," Literature Network, http://www.online-literature.com/london/49/ (accessed January 23, 2017).

6. *Twayne's*, p. 84.

7. Clarice Stasz, *American Dreamers: Charmian and Jack London* (New York: St. Martin's Press, 1988), p. 198.

8. New York Times, November 5, 1910, as quoted in John Perry, *Jack London: An American Myth* (Chicago: Nelson-Hall, 1981), p. 246.

9. Alex Kershaw, *Jack London: A Life* (New York: St. Martin's Press, 1997, p. 225.

10. The Valley of the Moon is the American Indian name for Sonoma Valley, California.

11. John Perry, *Jack London: An American Myth* (Chicago: Nelson-Hall, 1981), p. 297.

12. Ibid.

13. *San Francisco Chronicle*, November 23, 1916, as published in Perry, p. 300.

14. *Twayne's*, p. 82.

15. Ibid., pp. 128–129.

Chapter 11. London's Legacy

1. "Jack London's "Credo"," in Irving Shepard ed., *Jack London's Tales of Adventure* (New York: Doubleday, 1956), p. vii., http://london.sonoma.edu/credo.html.

2. "Jack London and the Great Earthquake and Fire," http://www.sfmuseum.org/hist5/jlondon.html (accessed November 23, 2016).

3. Jack London State Historic Park, http://www.jacklondonpark.com/ (accessed November 23, 2016).

4. Jack London International, http://www.jack-london.org/main_e.htm (November 23, 2016).

5. Brett & Kate McKay, "The Life of Jack London as a Case Study in the Power and Perils of Thumos — #1: Introduction," http://www.artofmanliness.com/2013/03/ 25/the-life-of-jack-london-as-a-case-study-in-thumos-1-introduction/ (accessed November 23, 2016).

6. Jack London Facebook Author Page, https://www.facebook.com/JackLondonAuthor (accessed November 23, 2016).

7. iLondon: The Immersive Jack London Experience, http://iclassicscollection.com/en/ilondon/ (accessed November 23, 2016). Part of the iClassics Collection. Released in 2016 to coincide with the 100th anniversary of London's death.

8. "Jack London: Beyond The Call of the Wild," *VQR, A National Journal of Literature & Discussion*, 2013, http://www.vqronline.org/jack-london-beyond-call-wild (accessed January 23, 2017).

Literary Terms

allegory A story that contains symbols and hidden meanings.

anthropomorphism Bestowing human traits on an animal.

bildungsroman A novel dealing with the education or development of a young protagonist who then takes his or her place in society as a mature or knowledgeable adult.

Darwinism The theory of evolution through natural selection popularized by Charles Darwin in his book *Origin of the Species.*

fable A story with a moral or lesson, often involving animals.

foil A character whose purpose is to serve as a contrast to another.

hero cycle A process of personal growth in which the person goes through several stages that require change. They are a call to adventure, departure, initiation, transformation, and return. The end result is a return to the point of origin with new information or new skills to benefit others.

hyperbole Bold overstatement for ironic or comic effect.

irony The use of words to express an idea or ideas that are the opposite of the words' literal meaning.

naturalism A style of fiction in which a character's life is determined strictly by his surroundings and genetics. The individual does not have a spirit but lives completely within the physical realm of nature.

paradox An idea or statement that contains contradictory elements.

protagonist The main character in a novel or other piece of writing.

serialization Publishing a story in parts at regular intervals. Magazines often serialized novels by printing a new chapter in each issue.

short story Fictional narrative prose that focuses on a single incident or a very short period of time.

tripartite soul Plato's division of the psyche into three parts: The appetitive mind, or physical desires, identified as the black horse on the left; the spirited (*thumos*) mind that seeks for high moral ground, identified as the white horse on the right; and the rational mind, the charioteer that (hopefully) keeps the chariot and horses under control.

Victorian Age The time of Queen Victoria's reign over the United Kingdom (1837–1901). Some novels of that time period were stories of romance in which the woman sought the perfect domestic life with the perfect man. The stories often included moral lessons of right and wrong, with appropriate justice administered to each class of character.

Major Works by Jack London

"Story of a Typhoon Off the Coast of Japan" (1893)
The Son of the Wolf (1900)
The God of His Fathers (1901)
Children of the Frost (1902)
A Daughter of the Snows (1902)
The Kempton–Wace Letters (1903)
The Call of the Wild (1903)
The People of The Abyss (1903)
The Sea-Wolf (1904)
Tales of the Fish Patrol (1905)
Moon-Face and Other Stories (1906)
White Fang (1906)
The Road (1907)
The Iron Heel (1908)
Martin Eden (1909)
Lost Face (1910)
Burning Daylight (1910)
Revolution and Other Essays (1910)
When God Laughs and Other Stories (1911)
The Cruise of the Snark (1911)
South Sea Tales (1911)
The House of Pride and Other Tales of Hawaii (1912)
The Night Born (1913)
John Barleycorn (1913)
The Valley of the Moon (1913)
The Scarlet Plague (1915)
The Star Rover (1915)
The Little Lady of the Big House (1916)
The Red One (1918)
On the Makaloa Mat (1919)
Jack London Reports (1979)

Further Reading

Books

Kershaw, Alex. *Jack London: A Life*. New York: St. Martin's Press, 1999.

Labor, Earle. *Jack London: An American Life*. New York: Farrar, Straus and Giroux, 2013.

Stasz, Clarice. *Jack London's Women*, reprint. Amherst, MA: University of Massachusetts Press, 2013.

Tichi, Cecilia. *Jack London: A Writer's Fight for a Better America*. Chapel Hill, NC: The University of North Carolina Press, 2015.

Websites

Jack London Educational Research Foundation
jacklondonfdn.org
Sponsors an annual descriptive writing contest for high school students to promote writing skills.

The Jack London Papers at the Huntington Library
huntington.org/WebAssets/Templates/content.aspx?id=10888
Starting page for research at the Huntington Library.

The Jack London Story and the Beauty Ranch
archive.org/details/londonbeautyranc00sheprich
Interview with Milo Shepard, London's great grandson, who recalls Charmian, his grandmother Eliza, and many historical details passed down relating to London.

Sonoma State University Jack London Collection
library.sonoma.edu/specialcollections/notable/london
Hub site for Jack London information, contains links to all London's works plus some of his personal correspondence with Charmian and famous people of the time.

INDEX